An Uncommon Soldier

An Uncommon Soldier

The Civil War Letters of Sarah Rosetta Wakeman,
alias Private Lyons Wakeman
153rd Regiment, New York State Volunteers

Edited by
Lauren Cook Burgess

with a Foreword by
James M. McPherson

Oxford University Press
New York   Oxford

Oxford University Press

Oxford   New York
Athens   Auckland   Bangkok   Bombay
Calcutta   Cape Town   Dar es Salaam   Delhi
Florence   Hong Kong   Istanbul   Karachi
Kuala Lumpur   Madras   Madrid   Melbourne
Mexico City   Nairobi   Paris   Singapore
Taipei   Tokyo   Toronto

and associated companies in
Berlin   Ibadan

Copyright © 1994 by Lauren Markland Cook Burgess

First published in 1994 by the MINERVA Center
Pasadena, MD

First issued as an Oxford University Press paperback, 1995

Oxford is a registered trademark of Oxford University Press

Library of Congress Cataloging-in-Publication Data
Wakeman, Sarah Rosetta.
An uncommon soldier : the Civil War letters of Sarah Rosetta
Wakeman, alias Pvt. Lyons Wakeman, 153rd Regiment, New York State
Volunteers, 1862–1864 / edited by Lauren Cook Burgess ; with
foreword by James M. McPherson.
p.   cm.3
Originally published: Pasadena, Md. : Minerva Center, 1994.
Includes bibliographical references (p.   ) and index.
ISBN 0-19-510243-6 (Pbk.)
1. Wakeman, Sarah Rosetta, 1843–1864—Correspondence. 2. United
States—History—Civil War, 1861–1865—Participation, Female.
3. United States—History—Civil War, 1861–1865–Personal
narratives. 4. United States. Army. New York Infantry Regiment,
153rd (1862–1865) 5. New York (State)—History—Civil War,
1861–1865—Personal narratives. 6. Women soldiers—New York
(State)—Afton Region—Correspondence. 7. Afton Region (N.Y.)—
Biography   I. Title.
E628.W35   1995
973.7′447—dc20   95-37251

2 4 6 8 10 9 7 5 3 1

Printed in the United States of America

Table of Contents

List of Illustrations

Acknowledgments

I am deeply grateful to many people whose contributions to this effort made it possible. First and foremost, my thanks are due to Mrs. Ruth Goodier for bringing her great-great-aunt's extraordinary letters to my attention, arranging her family's permission for publication, and for all of her cooperation, help, and good advice. Ruth Goodier's sister, Marjorie Ross, also helped with editing advice, as did John Goode of Bentonville Battleground and Dr. John David Smith of North Carolina State University. Curtis Alletore-Martin did an able job of copy editing the final draft.

DeAnne Blanton at the National Archives deserves a very special mention. She provided me with invaluable assistance, going beyond the call of duty to point me in productive research directions and to provide useful comments and suggestions on several drafts. Her friendship and support are highly valued.

Mr. Jackson K. Doane kindly provided background information and photographs of the original letters, daguerreotype, and ring whenever I made a request, and has my sincere appreciation for all of his help. Staff at the U.S. Army Military History Institute at Carlisle Barracks, the Library of Congress, the New York Historical Society, the Montgomery County (NY) Department of History and Archives (particularly Mrs. Violet Dake Fallone), the Chenango County Department of History and Archives, the Illinois State Historical Society, the Virginia Historical Society, the Louisiana State Archives, Chalmette National Cemetery, and other organizations and individuals too numerous to name were helpful with prompt responses to my requests for information.

Dr. Linda Grant De Pauw, Founder and President of The MINERVA Center, deserves special thanks for her faith in my ability to undertake this project and for publishing the final product. Her encouragement, comments, suggestions, and questions kept me motivated and led me to many new explorations and insights regarding women and the military in general, and Rosetta Wakeman and her army experiences in particular.

The MINERVA Center itself has my enduring gratitude for its role in promoting research and interest in women in the military--past, present, and future. It is a singular and difficult mission that the Center pursues to bring issues involving women and the military to the forefront in a society that has yet to fully recognize the significant contributions of hundreds of thousands of women who have always been there for their country in times of crisis, both to aid the cause and to serve and protect. Minerva publications and contacts have been a source of important information and insight throughout the course of this project.

I am deeply grateful to James M. McPherson, Edwin C. Bearss, Catherine Clinton, James I. Robertson, Jr., and Stephen W. Sears for their interest in the Wakeman letters. My sincere thanks also go to Connie Bond of *Smithsonian Magazine* and Eugene Meyer of *The Washington Post* for their dedication to making Rosetta's story known to the public.

Last, but by no means least, I am most thankful to my husband, Frederick Burgess. He has been a constant source of support and valuable advice for me while working on this project, and I have always been able to count on him to stand firm with me, shoulder to shoulder, when on the firing line.

Foreword

Civil War armies were the most literate in history to that time. More than 90 percent of the white Union soldiers and more than 80 percent of Confederate soldiers could read and write. Many of these three million soldiers were away from home for the first time during their military service. With strong ties to family and community, they stayed in touch by writing home and receiving letters in return --hundreds of millions of letters during the four years of war.

Unlike modern armies, those of the Civil War did not subject soldiers' letters to censorship. These letters are therefore extraordinarily candid and revealing about every facet of a soldier's life, from his opinion of officers and of political leaders to the boredom of life in winter quarters and the terrors of battle. Walt Whitman, a volunteer army nurse who heard the stories of hundreds of sick and wounded soldiers, wrote that "the real war will never get in the books." Perhaps not, in the sense that Whitman meant. But the real war did get into soldiers' letters, and through them into many books in which collections of these letters have been published. They are the best source for understanding the real war as experienced by the men who fought it.

Until now, however, we have had nothing comparable to help us understand the war as experienced by the women who fought. Yes, I said women. An estimated four hundred (the real number was probably larger) young women disguised themselves as men and easily finessed the superficial physical exams to enlist in Union and Confederate regiments. Their motives ranged from patriotism and love of adventure to a desire to stay with husbands or lovers who enlisted.

Some women soldiers were soon discovered and discharged. The usual reason for discovery was hospitalization for illness or wounds, as in the case of an Ohio private, Mary Scaberry, a.k.a. Charles Freeman, who was hospitalized for fever and subsequently discharged for "sexual incompatibility." Six female soldiers were found out when they had babies. As a male soldier in a Massachusetts regiment described one of these cases in a letter home: "there was an orderly in one of our regiments & he & the Corporal always slept together. Well, the other night the Corporal had a baby, for the Cpl. turned out to be a woman! She has been in 3 or 4 fights."

Some women soldiers served through the war without discovery. The most famous was Albert Cashier of the 95th Illinois Volunteer Infantry, whose name is inscribed on the Illinois monument at Vicksburg along with those of all other soldiers from the state who fought there. Cashier went to bachelor farming after the war, and not until an accident in 1911 required "his" hospitalization was it discovered that Albert Cashier was really Jennie Hodgers.

The editor of *An Uncommon Soldier* is a Civil War reenactor--a member of that large fraternity of at least 40,000 Americans who don replica blue or gray uniforms and pick up their replica Springfield rifled muskets to reenact Civil War battles and to serve as the essential extras in movies like *Glory* and *Gettysburg*. Like many of her Civil War predecessors, Lauren Cook Burgess was "caught" --when she was seen to emerge from the ladies room at Antietam National Battlefield Park during a reenactment in 1989. The National Park Service, citing the importance of "authenticity," banned her from impersonating a soldier for purposes of reenactment. But Burgess did not accept her discharge. Instead, she sued the Park Service for sex discrimination, and eventually won.

Her case divided the reenactment community. Sticklers for authenticity insisted that only males, including middle-aged, potbellied males, could pretend to be Civil War soldiers. Lauren Cook Burgess was not content to press her case only in the U.S. district court. She also appealed to the court of history. And there, also, she has triumphed. She has documented 135 women soldiers who served in the Union and Confederate armies, and her file continues to grow. Four women are known to have fought at Antietam; two were wounded and another killed there.

Publicity about Lauren Cook Burgess's second Battle of Antietam set in train a series of events that has produced the publication of these letters of *An Uncommon Soldier,* Sarah Rosetta Wakeman, a.k.a. Lyons Wakeman of the 153rd New York Volunteer Infantry. This is the first and, so far, the only collection of letters by a female soldier. But it probably will not be the last, as more letters will undoubtedly come to light to describe the war as experienced by women soldiers. In a splendid job of detective work, Burgess has learned a great deal about Rosetta Wakeman's life before and during her service in the 153rd. A superb introduction provides background and context for the letters, while crisp and unobtrusive annotation clarifies or adds important details. With the publication of *An Uncommon Soldier,* an important facet of the Civil War has finally gotten in the books.

James M. McPherson

Preface

Three years ago a letter from Mrs. Ruth Goodier arrived in my mailbox with the startling news that her "great-grandmother's older sister was a soldier in the Civil War. I have in my possession copies of her letters home and a copy of her photograph." Soon after, I was thrilled to read Sarah Rosetta Wakeman's letters for the first time.

Sometime after the Civil War, Wakeman's letters, a daguerreotype of her in uniform, and her engraved ring came to rest in an attic trunk in the home of her youngest sister's daughter. Mr. Jackson K. Doane, one of Rosetta's great-nephews, recalls talk about Rosetta, but, he says, "whenever I asked about her, my grandmother would kind of change the subject," although she did mention that she had a soldier sibling who went by the name of Lyons. Mr. Doane found the letters in his aunt's attic and read them in 1940 when he was young. Thereafter he returned often to the pine trunk to look through the letters and to speculate about their author.

In 1976, Mr. Doane was helping his aunt go through her attic. They discussed Rosetta's letters, and made the connection between Rosetta and Lyons, providing the link that led them to her enlisted name and army service record. Rosetta's secret subsequently became well known to the Wakeman family, and was included, along with her daguerreotype in uniform, in *Wakeman Genealogy II: A Sequel to Wakeman Genealogy I,* written by Thomas H. Wakeman and published in 1989. The original package of letters, picture, and engraved ring remain in the family's possession.

Rosetta Wakeman was far from well educated. While her handwriting was remarkably legible and working from good photocopies of the originals raised no serious problems, other editing challenges were legion. Her punctuation was virtually nonexistent, rendering her letters one long, run-on sentence; her capitalization of words was erratic; and, although spellings were not yet standardized in the mid-nineteenth century, her spelling was more dependent on how she heard or spoke words than on anything she learned in school.

For example, she consistently spelled "you" as "yow," "here" as "hear," and so on, and her spelling of unfamiliar words was even more tortured. In one letter she spelled "barracks" as "barrict," in another as "bairock," and in yet another circumstance, "Barouck." "Alexandria" in her lexicon was "Alexdary," "Alexdrany," and finally, after several months spent there, "Alexandria."

Because Rosetta's lack of punctuation, erratic capitalization, and distorted phonetic spelling would render her letters confusing and nearly unfathomable to most modern readers, some of these things have been corrected in the version presented here. The following editing conventions are used:

> Punctuation is inserted to separate sentences, and sentence openings are capitalized. Other capitalizations (or lack thereof) within sentences are retained. Where there is the possibility of another interpretation of sentence breaks or punctuation, a footnote contains the original.

> Most spellings are changed to conform to modern standards and to the real names of actual people and places, with one notable exception: where Rosetta's original grammar would have been disturbed, her spelling is retained. Many words that she split, i.e., "in Joy" and "a bought," are combined, except for "my Self" and "you[r] self." Where a misspelled word is open to interpretation, a footnote appears containing the original spelling. Where her meaning is not clear, the original is retained in italics.

> Paragraph breaks are inserted where a new thought begins or when an addendum was made to a letter. The material is also organized into three chronological chapters.

> Significant words and phrases that are crossed out in the original letters are contained in footnotes. An occasional dropped word or word ending is inserted in the text in brackets.

> Date line openings of each letter are standardized as much as possible. Several undated fragments were found among the letters, and are included here with a note to that effect. In all of these cases, the fragments are placed among the dated letters whose content most closely matches that

which is discussed in the fragment, or in the order in which they were originally found.

Rosetta's original grammar is retained throughout the letters, including her occasional neglect of the past tense and possessive forms, her frequent failure to make nouns and verbs agree, and her odd use of the word "you" instead of "your."

Where possible, individuals and historically significant places and events alluded to in the letters are identified. Chapter introductions and comments designed to put the material in context are in italics, as are supplementary and corroborative material from the 153rd New York State Volunteer's Regimental Orders and Letter books. Two letters from Rosetta's cousin Frank Roberts that were found with her package and reference Wakeman also appear. Photographic material, documents, and maps are included to add to the reader's knowledge of Rosetta Wakeman's life and times in the Union army.

Rosetta's writing has not been changed and is completely her own. The editorial changes described above are intended solely to make the reader's comprehension of Rosetta's meaning clearer and more easily grasped than would otherwise be the case. Photocopies of the letters are available for review in the Library of Congress.

Lauren Cook Burgess
Fayetteville, North Carolina
February, 1994

Introduction

What transforms the letters of Pvt. Lyons Wakeman from merely interesting reading into a unique and fascinating addition to Civil War literature is who wrote them--for Private Wakeman was not what "he" seemed to be. The five-foot tall soldier's true identity was that of a simple young farm girl from central New York state named Sarah Rosetta Wakeman.

For reasons that are only glimpsed in her letters, Rosetta Wakeman decided to leave her home in Afton, New York and disguise herself as a man sometime in early August of 1862. She secured a position as a coal handler on a canal boat, but at the end of her first trip up the Chenango Canal she encountered recruiters for the 153rd New York State Volunteers. Wakeman enlisted for three years or the duration of the war. For the next two years, she would serve as a private in the Union army, using the name Lyons Wakeman.

Although Rosetta did not survive the war, she did leave behind an unusual record of her military service in the form of letters written to her family. Preserved in an attic for over a century by family members who considered her somewhat of a black sheep and her adventures in male attire a bit strange, Rosetta's unique collection of letters have only recently emerged in the public light.

Private Wakeman was not alone in embarking on her strange adventure, however. Hundreds of women, North and South, disguised themselves as men and enlisted in the armies of our nation's great sectional conflict. They cut their hair short, donned pants, and gave themselves male aliases. They endured the hardships and horrors of Civil War army life, serving undetected at the sides of their male comrades. Their reasons for doing so were as varied as their backgrounds and the hometowns from which they came. They enlisted to be with a husband or loved one, or, like many of their male counterparts, for the sheer adventure and romance of joining the army and seeing places far from home. Some women adopted male attire and signed up to earn the bounties and pay offered to enlistees. Many enlisted out of patriotism, to serve their respective countries and their causes. Dressing as men was, for these women, a means to an end--they did so to strike a solid blow against the enemy, or to gain a measure of economic, legal, and social independence unavailable to them as women.

In the massive *History of Woman Suffrage,* Susan B. Anthony, Elizabeth Cady Stanton, and Matilda Gage noted that "army regulations" were used as an excuse to deny recognition of these women soldiers, and that historians "made no mention of women's services during the war," though

> *Hundreds of women marched steadily up to the mouth of a hundred cannon pouring out fire and smoke, shot and shell, mowing down the advancing hosts like grass; men, horses, and colors going down in confusion, disappearing in clouds of smoke; the only sound, the screaming of shells, the crackling of musketry, the thunder of artillery . . . through all this women were sustained by the enthusiasm born of love of country and liberty.*[1]

In her post-war memoirs, Mary Livermore of the U.S. Sanitary Commission wrote that "the number of women soldiers known to the service . . . [is] little less than four hundred," although she herself was convinced that "a larger number of women disguised themselves and enlisted in the service, for one cause or other, than was dreamed of."[2] If army officials and most historians took no notice of the contributions made by these women in the ranks, the popular press did, and many accounts of women soldiers that survive today come from newspapers of the period. Indeed, one chronicler wrote that during the war, "accounts presented themselves almost daily to the eye, of the valorous deeds of females fighting in the ranks for months, without their sex being divulged."[3]

Even if the estimate of 400 women soldiers is accepted as an upper limit, it is an astonishing figure, notwithstanding the fact that over three million American men served in armies and navies during the Civil War. How were so many women able to accomplish this incredible deception, when it is inconceivable that a woman could enter the military under the same circumstances today?

First of all, army recruitment physical examinations during the Civil War were only as good as the surgeon who performed them.

A recruit was unlikely to face an exam more rigorous than holding out his hands to demonstrate that he had a working trigger finger, or perhaps opening his mouth to show that his teeth were strong enough to rip open a minie ball cartridge. Sarah Edmonds, alias Pvt. Franklin Thompson, described her army medical exam as "a firm handshake" with an inquiry about "Frank's" occupation.[4]

Furthermore, army life in the 1860s differed significantly from the modern military. The soldiers who formed the rank and file early in the Civil War were led by volunteer officers, most of whom had as much to learn about military life as those under their command. There was no boot camp with intensive physical training as there is today. And, although living and sleeping arrangements were as close or closer than today's standard, the fact that the majority of soldiers lived outside throughout the war, with the latitude to wash and attend to sanitary matters out of sight of comrades, made it possible for females in the ranks to avoid the scrutiny that would give them away. Societal standards of modesty ensured that no one would question a shy soldier's reluctance to bathe in a river with his messmates or to relieve himself in the open company sinks.

A second, and very large, advantage for 19th century women was that gender identification in the Victorian age was more closely linked to attire and other superficial appearances than to physical characteristics. Voluminous hoop skirts were the order of the day for women, who wore their long hair in elaborate arrangements. A woman in pants in 1861 was a sight more rare than a man wearing a dress is today. Thus, if it wore pants, most people of the period would naturally have assumed that the person was a man. In polite society, speculating further or inquiring upon what lay beneath another person's attire would mark the questioner as less than a gentleman or a lady.[5]

Broad acceptance of a person based on superficial appearances led to many interesting comments that reveal the naivete of Civil War soldiers regarding the women secreted among them. Capt. Ira B. Gardner of the 14th Maine enrolled a soldier in his company who served for two years before he realized she was female. Wrote Gardner, "I did not learn of her sex until the close of the war. If I had been anything but a *boy,* I should probably have seen from her form that she was a female [emphasis added]."[6] Robert Hodges, a Confederate soldier, related this story in a letter home: "One of the soldiers directed my attention to a youth apparently about seventeen years of age well dressed with a lieutenant's badge on his collar. I remarked I saw nothing strange. He then told me the young man was not a man but a female.''[7] Members of the famous Pvt. Franklin Thompson's brigade referred to ''him'' as ''Our Woman'' because of ''his'' feminine mannerisms and ''ridiculously small boots.''[8] But even so, many of her comrades testified after the war that they never suspected that the private was anything other than a ''he.''

A common element of women soldiers' stories is their ability to recognize other women in the ranks while the men around them were oblivious to their female comrades' deception. This suggests strongly that, while women knew what to look for in order to recognize other women in male attire, the men around them were either unfamiliar with the sight of women in pants or had extreme difficulty accepting the possibility that a fellow soldier might not be male. Certainly, the ill-fitting uniforms of the Civil War armies helped to conceal feminine physical characteristics, but a reluctance to accept that a female was a soldier must have been operating, particularly in cases where women served for very long periods of time without discovery. Biases about the physical, emotional, and intellectual abilities of women, as well as beliefs about appropriate and acceptable feminine roles, precluded the concept of a female soldier and rendered many men in the armies incapable of recognizing the women among them.

Yet a third circumstance enabled women to blend into the ranks with their male comrades. A large number of young and beardless boys whose voices had yet to change served in both the Confederate and Federal armed forces, and the armies of the Civil War were youthful in the main.[9] The presence of pre-adolescent boys in the ranks unintentionally aided the likewise beardless and high-voiced women to go undetected.

Women soldiers were often discovered when treated for wounds or illness. In several cases, death on the field of battle or capture by the enemy revealed the combatant as a woman. Clara Barton nursed a woman at Antietam, discovering the shy soldier's secret only because her tunic was removed to treat a chest wound.[10] Another angel of mercy, Annie Wittenmyer, wrote in her memoirs of befriending a woman soldier in the hospital at Chattanooga. She had served for a year in the western army, and was discovered when she was wounded, captured, and returned through the lines by Confederates during the Battle of Chickamauga.[11] One brave woman in gray, who probably took part in Pickett's Charge during the Battle of Gettysburg, was found dead on the field by a burial detail.[12]

No fewer than six pregnant women went undiscovered until they delivered babies. A ''Confederate Officer'' had a ''bouncing baby boy'' while a prisoner of war at Johnson's Island, Ohio.[13] One woman, who belonged to a nine-month regiment, went into labor while on picket duty and produced a ''fine, fat recruit.''[14] Another soldier caused Col. Elijah H.C. Cavins to write home that "a corporal was promoted to sergeant for gallant conduct at the battle of Fredericksburgh--since which time the sergeant has become the mother of a child. What use have we for women, if soldiers in the army can give birth to children? It is said that the sergeant and *his* Capt. occupied the same tent, they being intimate friends [emphasis added]."[15]

A common myth is that women soldiers were ugly or mannish in appearance. Some women were quite attractive, and they still managed to deceive the men around them. One soldier's letter home from a hospital near Gettysburg mentioned a ''female secesh here'' who was ''very good looking.'' She had taken part in the battle, was wounded, and subsequently lost a leg to amputation.[16] Upon meeting two women who had been found in his command, Maj. Gen. Philip Sheridan remarked that one of them was ''comely,'' so much so that he couldn't understand how she had successfully impersonated a man.[17]

Many served for years and were not revealed as women until long after the cessation of hostilities. In a deposition for the Pension Bureau investigation of Albert D.J. Cashier, one former messmate said that ''While I was in the service I did not dream that he was a woman, but we used to talk about his not having any *beard* [emphasis added].'' The diminutive, five-foot tall Albert was also described as ''the shortest man in the company'' but nevertheless ''a brave little soldier.'' Cashier served out an entire three-year enlistment despite the fact that ''his'' real identity was that of an Irish immigrant named Jennie Hodgers.[18] In many cases like Private Cashier's, it seems that regardless of a woman's physical appearance, her male comrades assumed she was, literally, one of the boys.

Women who enlisted as soldiers did so in secrecy. Because of this, the historical record of the military service they rendered their countries is necessarily incomplete. Usually only a husband or brother knew the true identity of a woman enlistee. A single woman did not have even that aid and comfort in the predominantly male world she became a part of upon entering military service. Women who joined the army often feared discovery as much for the label of loose morals they would earn as for the embarrassment of dismissal from service. A woman's reputation was virtually her only possession that middle- and upper-class society valued. Being returned to petticoats without that important possession spelled potential disgrace and ruin for those who chose to serve their countries in a nontraditional role. Women who followed a husband, sweetheart, or brother into the army, or who cited burning patriotism as their reason for signing up, rather than a desire for independence and adventure, received more favorable press when their stories became public. Although most accounts were neutral or complementary, some newspaper reports about women discovered in the ranks implied that they were of very bad character, indeed.

An example is the case of Mary and Mollie Bell, alias Pvts. Tom Parker and Bob Morgan. These sisters were discovered and arrested while under Lt. Gen. Jubal Early's command after serving for two years. An October, 1864 *Richmond Enquirer* article stated that they were detained for "demoralizing" Early's veterans, which has been interpreted to mean that they were prostitutes.[19] The *Enquirer's* editorial slant and the subsequent interpretations by historians ignore the fact that Mary and Molly could not have escaped detection for two years if they had been engaged in the "ancient trade," the latter a common, but erroneous, assumption made about women soldiers.[20] Poor Mollie Bean served in the 47th North Carolina for two years and was twice wounded, only for the *Richmond Whig* to report her arrest and confinement in Castle Thunder Prison, "that common receptacle of the guilty, the suspected, and the unfortunate. This poor creature is, from her record, manifestly crazy."[21]

Even that most famous of women Civil War soldiers, Sarah Emma E. Edmonds, failed to mention in her 1864 memoirs that her nursing and spying exploits were undertaken while she was serving in the 2nd Michigan Volunteers as a man. Edmonds kept that piece of information about Pvt. Franklin Thompson a closely held secret for many years after the war until she and her husband fell on hard times. Then Emma, disabled by a war injury, successfully requested an 1886 act of Congress to remove the charge of desertion from her military record so that she could claim her soldier pension. Her need for monetary assistance outweighed her justified fear of the ugly rumors and talk that accompanied her public acknowledgement that she had served in McClellan's army in male disguise.[22]

For those women who resumed their female identities after the war, fear of society's condemnation of their exploits made them shy away from public notoriety due to their army service. For those who chose after the war to continue the relative freedom afforded them by living as men, maintaining secrecy was of utmost necessity upon leaving the ranks. For those women who were discovered and discharged during the war, or who revealed their true identity in order to leave the army, newspaper and other reports rarely give more than vague clues as to these women warriors' true identities and military exploits.

There is also a dearth of documentation such as women soldiers' letters and diaries, which may in part be related to the distinctly different roles and behavior allowed 19th-century American women depending on their class or social station. Rural and frontier farming women knew how to handle a horse, a rifle, a hoe, and their liquor in order to survive. Poor immigrant women from the cities worked at hard, physical labor and possessed none of the refined sensibilities of their ''betters.'' Women such as these, who were confident of their survival skills, would have few qualms about their ability to measure' up with the men in the military. An educated, well-mannered young lady, however, would be less likely to don soldier's garb because it was contrary to her upbringing and life expectations. Indeed, among the documented cases of women combatants for whom background information is known, the majority were from poor and agrarian classes, where education levels and rates of literacy were low.[23] The fact that poor and rural women were unable or less disposed to write letters and diaries may account for the apparent lack of such documentation of women's Civil War military service.

In this sense, Rosetta Wakeman is probably representative of the majority of the women who fought for the blue and the gray, much more so than the well-educated Sarah Edmonds. Rosetta's record of her soldier experiences is also representative of the great majority of men who served as common soldiers in the Civil War, whose less literary letters and diaries are rarely, if ever, published.

Because most reports available regarding Civil War female soldiers are sketchy at best, there remains a great deal of mystery and controversy surrounding them. A vast amount of research is required to satisfactorily document the wartime experiences of the women warriors mentioned briefly in newspapers, official documents, letters, diaries, and memoirs. Only two women soldiers wrote published memoirs of their army service, and only one of these memoirs, that of Sarah Emma E. Edmonds, has been confirmed as a substantially true account through biographical research.[24]

Viewed in this perspective, the letters home of Sarah Rosetta Wakeman are all the more valuable. They represent the only unvarnished, contemporary account of a woman's experiences as a soldier during the Civil War to come to light.

But the most stunning fact about Rosetta Wakeman's letters is that they exist at all, and that they survived. The stubborn independence Rosetta displayed by leaving home to find her own fortune would have caused a permanent rift with all but the most free-thinking or rock-solid of mid-nineteenth century families. That Rosetta's family was able to accept her enormous break from convention--to take a man's name and a man's place in the army--speaks volumes for their love and concern for her. Not only did her family correspond with her, but they told other family and friends how to find her so that they might write or visit her. All who knew and cared for Rosetta must have felt much like the family and friends of modern women who have broken the bonds of tradition to pursue ''unfeminine'' careers and goals--perhaps a bit mortified and frightened, but nevertheless proud of their loved one. The fact that her letters, picture, and ring were carefully preserved and packed away to survive down the years also speak to a family's pride and love, even though family members referred to Rosetta as a ''brother'' after the war, undoubtedly to avoid long and difficult explanations.[25]

Sarah Rosetta Wakeman was born on January 16, 1843, the eldest daughter of Harvey Anable and Emily Hale Wakeman. The Wakeman's had eight more children after Rosetta's birth, totaling seven girls and two boys.

According to the 1850 Census, Harvey and his family lived in the southern half of Bainbridge town in Chenango County, which later subdivided into the town of Afton. Chenango County could not ''point to any gigantic commercial or manufacturing enterprise within [its] borders,'' but it could, ''with just pride, refer the stranger to the no less gratifying evidences of wealth, prosperity and contentment exhibited by the tillers of the soil.''[26] The principal geographical feature of the township of Afton, named for a small river in Ayrshire, England, was the Susquehanna River. The hills and valleys were ''very productive and generally susceptible to cultivation to their summits.'' The soil was ''well adapted to corn, tobacco, and hops,'' but primarily Afton was ''a dairy town, nearly every farmer keeping as many cows as his land will subsist. . .''[26]

On the 1850 Census, Rosetta is listed as seven years old and as having attended some school in the past year. The 1860 Census shows her as seventeen years old and also as attending some school in the previous year. Her occupation is listed as a ''domestic.'' From family records, it appears that the Wakemans lived southwest of Afton town near the Broome County border, making Harpersville the Post Office closest to their homestead and the place to which Rosetta posted her letters. Harvey Wakeman's father and family were from Harpersville, and his brother, John Wakeman, lived there.[28] Harvey's attention was not all focused across the county border, however. He qualified for and was elected to one of Afton's four Constable positions in 1858, indicating that he was well-known and respected in town.[29]

Rosetta's letters give only a few clues as to why she left home in early August 1862, dressed as a man, and signed on as a Chenango Canal boatman. Her father had incurred debt, enough to cause Rosetta some concern. At 19 years of age, Rosetta appeared to have no prospects for marriage, which would have relieved the family of her care. No doubt she helped her father work the farm. But her farm work would have been of limited value in paying Harvey Wakeman's debt, and her position as a domestic could not have paid enough to substantially assist her family. Like other women before her who faced similar family situations or worse, Rosetta realized that one of the only ways open to finding an honorable position that paid enough for her to assist her indebted family was by dressing and acting the part of a man. She wrote that "I knew that I could help you more to leave home than to stay there with you." Indeed, after joining the army, Rosetta sent home substantial sums of money, in amounts that she could not have earned as quickly in any position open to her as a woman, with the possible exception of prostitution.[30]

In addition to money, debt, and Rosetta's feelings of responsibility for her family, there was the issue of how she got along with family members. "I want to drop all old affray* and I want you to do the same, and when I come home we will be good friends as ever," she pled in her first letter home. There is a passing reference to a less-than-ideal relationship with her sister Lois, and a request for her family to forgive her "for everything I ever did," and she will forgive them the same.

Rosetta frequently addressed her mother with reassurances that her affections for her family were as strong as ever, as evidenced by the money and gifts she sent home. For her father, Rosetta had questions about his farming pursuits, land purchases, and other business. Rosetta's high level of interest in her father's farming, her knowledge of the details of the family farm, and her desire to own her own farm after the war are evidence that she served as her father's farmhand. Being the eldest in a family whose first male

---

An archaic term meaning public brawl or fight.

child was elementary school age, it is likely that Rosetta provided a great deal of assistance to her father. Perhaps she became accustomed to wearing male clothes while working on the farm.

Throughout her letters, Rosetta's mixed feelings about her home and family are evident. She flatly states that she is "quit of home and will never live there again," will dress as she pleases, and will make new friends wherever she goes. She also says that she would be "aShamed to Come" home, most likely a reference to her fear of what home folks would think of her unconventional adventures. At the same time her longing for home, family, and friends and her desire to be back among them is a constant theme. She wants to have her own farm far away when the war is over, but she also wants her family to prepare for her return. Rosetta's ambivalence on this score is very modern. Her story--that of a woman determined to do what she wants, to seek adventure and a new life regardless of what people think, and the impact her course of action has on family relationships--has much in it that latter-day women and men will recognize.

Once Rosetta made the decision to become a "man," she set off to the nearest big city, Binghamton, to look for a job. There she worked "for half a month" for $4.00 pay. Then she signed on to do manual labor on a coal barge at $20.00 for four trips up the Chenango Canal, which bisected central New York from Binghamton in the south to Utica in the north. At the end of her first trip she encountered soldiers who urged her to sign up with the 153rd Regiment, New York State Volunteers. The $152.00 bounty offered to enlistees in the 153rd was over a year's worth of wages to even the "male" Rosetta.

Reporting her name as "Lyons" Wakeman and inflating her age to 21, Rosetta enrolled in the 153rd on August 30, 1862. On the regimental descriptive roll she is listed as five feet tall, fair complected, with brown hair, blue eyes, and an occupation of "boatman." The newly-forming 153rd stayed in the Montgomery County locale until its ranks were filled with recruits. The regiment was mustered into United States service on October 17, 1862 at Fonda, New York, and embarked for Washington on October 18. Pvt. Lyons Wakeman's army career had begun.

On arriving in Washington on October 22, the 153rd Regiment was sent to perform provost marshal and guard duty in Alexandria, Virginia, as part of the extensive defenses of Washington City. While posted there for nine months, the 153rd was often aroused from sleep and formed in line of battle across the approaches to

Washington in order to repel expected attacks. On one occasion the regiment was kept behind temporary barriers, anticipating the enemy, for 14 consecutive days and nights.[31]

On July 20, 1863, the 153rd was transferred to Washington to guard against expected draft riots similar to those that occurred in New York City on July 14. The regiment was assigned to barracks on Capitol hill, which the 153rd's chaplain attributed to "our excellence in discipline [which] has no doubt assigned us this position of honor under the dome of the Capitol and nearer to it than any other Regiment."[32] The 153rd guarded the depot of the Baltimore and Ohio Railroad, patrolled the city, conveyed troops to the front and prisoners to the prisoner of war camp at Point Lookout, Maryland, and guarded the "contraband," or ex-slave refugee camp, as well as the central guard house and Carroll and Old Capitol Prisons. While in Washington, the 153rd witnessed the completion of the Capitol dome, and saw "the Goddess of Liberty completed and placed in position upon the capitol, and [heard] the thunder of a hundred guns as they belched forth their welcome from the surrounding fortifications."[33]

In late February 1864, the 153rd was transferred to the field to take part in Maj. Gen. Nathaniel P. Banks' ill-fated Red River Campaign in Louisiana. The campaign commenced on March 15 in Franklin, west of New Orleans, from whence Banks' army marched toward Shreveport by way of Alexandria, then Natchitoches, and then Sabine Cross Roads, where they met a Confederate force with dire results. In a post-war speech, Lt. George H. Hodges of the 153rd proclaimed that, "No tongue can tell nor pen indite the hardships . . . endured on that march of over seven hundred miles through an enemies country, where with a scarcity of water, any slough was sought for with eagerness, and though animals partly decomposed and reeking with their millions of parasites were floating upon its surface, [the regiment was] obliged to drink its waters to allay the thirst caused by that southern sun."[34] Bad water, bad army diet, and almost 700 miles of hard marching and fighting in hot, humid Louisiana bayou and hill country wreaked havoc on unacclimated troops like the 153rd, who were said by one veteran of the campaign to sicken and die by the thousands.[35]

Private Wakeman finally met the enemy on the field of battle, and "received [her] initial fire and felt the dread realities of war"[36] on April 9, 1864 at Pleasant Hill, the second major engagement during the Red River campaign. There the 153rd "stood calmly at [its] post amid a shower of shot and shell, pouring volley after volley of leaden hail into the enemy, and repulsing six desperate charges of [Maj. Gen.] Dick Taylor's victorious troop who left the ground strewn with their dead and wounded comrades."[37] Although the 153rd's first battle successfully checked Confederate forces, Banks' army was forced to retreat back down the Red River, becoming engaged once more at Monett's Bluff before they again reached Alexandria, Louisiana.

With the end of the campaign almost in sight, Rosetta developed chronic diarrhea, which struck her down along with many of her other comrades who had been plunged from soft garrison duty into active campaigning in an inhospitable climate. While at Alexandria, Private Wakeman reported to the regimental hospital on May 3, and was transferred to Marine U.S.A. General Hospital in New Orleans, where she arrived on May 22. Her condition was listed as acute by the time she reached New Orleans. After a month of hospitalization she died on June 19, 1864, leaving no record of having been discovered.[38]

Like many of her male counterparts, Rosetta Wakeman came from a modest and unsophisticated rural background. Her letters contain none of the romance or expression of high ideals found in the better-educated Sarah Edmonds' account of her service to the Union. Nor was Rosetta's regiment involved in the war's most crucial military engagements, although she twice took part in battle. Her observations focused on her immediate surroundings rather than the enormous events swirling around her. She was more curious about her father's farming and news of friends from home than she was about the great questions resolved on the bloody battlefields of the Civil War.

Rosetta did, however, evince a simple determination to perform honorably the duty required of a soldier. In this regard, she differed not at all from her male comrades who volunteered early in the war. Private Wakeman also expressed her pride in her ability to drill, stand on the firing line, and perform a soldier's duties as well as anyone else.

Her letters give us glimpses of wartime Washington, D.C., and of the daily routine of the troops garrisoned there. And when transferred to the field to take part in the Red River Campaign, Rosetta wrote of hard marching and combat--but was more concerned about relaying news of wounded comrades to those at home. Once in the field, she became conscientious about signing her letters as "Edwin R. Wakeman," another male alias she assumed,* no

---

* She began signing her letters with "Edwin R." in 1863. It is possible that she did so because of her admiration of the 153rd's Colonel, Edwin P. Davis.

doubt due to fear that she would be revealed and discharged if her letters fell into the wrong hands. As her service wore on, the tone of her letters became more fatalistic, and her faith in God and the afterlife, where she would meet her family and friends again, became a commonly expressed and comforting theme.

Numerous questions remain about Private Wakeman. Did she truly deceive her comrades, or did they come to accept her as one of the boys? What problems, if any, did her disguise or her sex cause her? These and other questions remain in the realm of speculation, as is so often the case with women soldiers. It is notable that her perceptions of army life and war are remarkably similar to those of hundreds of thousands of men who served in the Civil War military. Indeed, the reader must remain sensitive to Rosetta's true identity in order to catch many of the gender-related nuances in her letters.

A substantial amount of corroborating and supplementary information from the 153rd New York's regimental records and other sources is included with the letters to flesh out the full story of Rosetta's army service. The version presented here is faithful to Private Wakeman's originals, including her habit of writing and signing numerous addenda to her missives. The personality of Rosetta Wakeman is evident in every letter, with all of her bluntness, bravado, independence, pride, faith, and occasional reflectiveness, giving the reader a unique insight into the strength of character and the fearlessness of one woman who flaunted convention and dared to enlist as a soldier during the Civil War.

Here, then, is the story of one woman soldier's service to the Union during the War of Rebellion, told as she experienced it. She did her duty honorably, and expected and received no special treatment because of her sex. She volunteered to render her country her "last full measure of devotion," and ultimately it did cost Rosetta her life. For that, Private Wakeman, and women like her, deserve the same honor and respect that we accord all other veterans of that tragic conflagration that ripped through America over a century ago.

NOTES

1. Susan B. Anthony, Matilda Gage, and Elizabeth Cady Stanton, *History of Woman Suffrage,* Vol. II (New York, NY: Fowler & Wells, 1882), p. 21.

2. Mary Livermore, *My Story of the War* (Hartford, CT: A.D. Worthington & Co., 1888), pp. 120-121.

3. Fazar Kirkland, *Reminiscences of the Blue and Gray, 1861 to 1865,* (Chicago: Preston Publishing Co., [1866]1895), p. 173.

4. May 26, 1883, *Detroit Post and Tribune* interview with Sarah Emma E. Edmonds, as quoted in Sylvia Dannett, *She Rode with the Generals,* (New York: Thomas Nelson & Sons, 1960), p. 52.

5. An example of the latter is presented by Mary Livermore, who was approached by an officer of the 19th Illinois Infantry on a "delicate" matter. The officer suspected that one of his men was not quite right, but was reluctant to broach the subject with the individual without additional confirmation and assistance. Livermore agreed with the officer's speculation that one of his men was, indeed, a woman, and agreed to take charge of her. Livermore, *My Story of the War*, pp. 113-114.

6. Ira B. Gardner, *Recollections of a Boy Member of the Maine 14th,* (Lewiston, ME: Lewiston Journal Co., 1902), p. 24.

7. Robert Hodges, Jr. (Maury Darst, ed.), "Robert Hodges, Jr., Confederate Soldier," *East Texas Historical Journal,* Vol. 9, No. 1, pp. 37-38.

8. May 26, 1883, *Detroit Post and Tribune* interview with Damon Stewart, former member of the 2nd Michigan Volunteers, as quoted in Dannett, p. 247.

9. Bell I. Wiley, *The Life of Billy Yank* (Baton Rouge and London: Louisiana State Univ. Press, [1952] 1990), pp. 296-303.

10. Post-war speech by Clara Barton, 1866, quoted in Elizabeth Brown Pryor, *Clara Barton: Professional Angel,* (Philadelphia: Univ. of Pennsylvania Press, 1987), p. 99.

11. Annie Wittenmyer, *Under the Guns: A Woman's Reminiscences of the Civil War,* (Boston: Stillings & Co., 1895), pp. 17-20.

12. *Official Records of the War of the Rebellion,* Report of Gen. Hays on Gettysburg burials. Series I, Vol. 27, Part 1, p. 378.

13. December 12, 1864, Sandusky, Ohio *Register* as quoted in Bell I. Wiley, *Confederate Women,* (Westport, CT: Greenwood Press, 1975), p. 142.

14. Col. Adrian R. Root, 94th New York State Volunteers, to parents, April 5, 1863. Courtesy B.R. Maryniak, Buffalo, NY.

15. Barbara A. Smith, ed., *The Civil War Letters of Col. Elijah H.C. Cavins, 14th Indiana,* (Owensboro, KY: Cook-McDowell Publications, 1981), p. 132.

16. Thomas Read, 5th Michigan, to parents, August 20, 1863, Univ. of Michigan Library, as quoted in Gregory A. Coco, *On the Bloodstained Field,* (The Wheatfield Press, 1987), p. 40.

17. Philip H. Sheridan, *Civil War Memoirs,* (New York: Webster & Co., 1888), p. 253.

18. Record Group 15, Records of the Veterans Administration, Pension File #C-2, 573248, based on the service of Pvt. Albert D.J. Cashier, 95th Illinois Infantry, National Archives.

19. October 31, 1864 *Richmond Enquirer,* as quoted in Mary Elizabeth Massey, *Bonnet Brigades,* (New York: Alfred A. Knopf, 1966), p. 84; and James I. Robertson, Jr., *Soldiers Blue and Gray,* (Columbia, SC: Univ. of South Carolina Press, 1988), p. 119.

20. It is unlikely that a woman would go to the trouble of disguising herself as a man and enlisting, in secrecy, only to reveal herself to her comrades as she would have to do in order to practice prostitution. It is particularly unlikely when one considers that there were other positions with the Civil War armies open to women, in attire and circumstances more suited to the oldest profession. Both Union and Confederate military regulations allowed for up to four *women* per company to serve as laundresses, meaning that up to 40 women could have accompanied a standard-sized regiment. War Department of the Confederate States of America, *Regulations for the Army of the Confederate States of America, 1863,* (Richmond, VA: J.W. Randolph, 1863), pp. 12, 77, 192, 195, 198, 237, and 238-239; War Department of the United States, *Revised Regulations for the Army of the United States,* (Philadelphia: J.G.L. Brown, 1861), pp. 24, 35, 112, 132-133, 284, and 343.

21. February 20, 1865 *Richmond Whig* as quoted in Weymouth T. Jordan, Jr., *North Carolina Troops in the Civil War: 1861-1865, A Roster,* Vol. XI, Infantry, (Raleigh, NC: Division of Archives & History, 1987), p. 363.

22. Edmonds to Richard Halsted, January 27, 1885, as quoted in Dannett, pp. 264-265; and Julie Wheelwright, *Amazons and Military Maids: Women Who Dressed as Men in the Pursuit of Life, Liberty, & Happiness,* (London: Pandora Press, 1989), pp. 137-138.

23. Among the 135 women who enlisted as soldiers for whom references and documentation are available, background information exists for 12 female soldiers. Nine of the twelve came from rural farm families or poor and immigrant backgrounds.

24. Sara Emma E. Edmonds, *Nurse & Spy,* (Hartford, CT: W.S. Williams & Co., 1864) and Loreta Janeta Velasquez, *The Woman in Battle,* (Hartford, CT: T. Belknap, 1876). Some incidents in Velasquez's fanciful memoirs can be confirmed through other sources, but the work is generally considered to be fiction. Sarah Edmonds' 1864 army memoirs tell a substantially true story, as established by Sylvia Dannett in her Edmonds biography, *She*

Rode with the Generals. The Lady Lieutenant: The Strange and Thrilling Adventures of Madeline Moore, (Philadelphia: Barclay & Co., 1862) is another supposedly fictional woman soldier memoir about General McClellan's 1861 West Virginia Campaign.

25. Ida Neva Smith, daughter of Catherine Wakeman, *Letters, 1976.* Courtesy Mrs. Ruth Goodier, Chipley, Florida.

26. James A. Smith, *History of Chenango and Madison Counties,* (Syracuse, NY: D. Mason & Co., 1880), p. 83.

27. James A. Smith, p. 134.

28. Thomas H. Wakeman, *Wakeman Genealogy 1630-1899,* (Meriden, CT: Journal Publishing Co., 1900), pp. 209, 262.

29. James A. Smith, p. 142.

30. For an excellent discussion and analysis of the largely pre-20th century phenomenon of women who wore male attire and presented themselves to society as men, see Julie Wheelwright, *Amazons & Military Maids: Women Who Dressed as Men in the Pursuit of Life, Liberty & Happiness.*

31. F.W. Beers & Co., *History of Montgomery and Fulton Counties (NY),* (New York: Geo. McNamara , Printer, 1878), pp. 178-184. September 17, 1914 Fonda, NY *Morning Herald,* "History of the 153rd N.Y.S.V.".

32. Chaplain Jacob H. Enders, 153rd New York State Volunteers, to sister, July 23, 1863. *Letters, 1862-1881.* Montgomery County Department of History and Archives, Fonda, New York.

33. *Record of the 153rd New York State Infantry,* read by Lt. George H. Hodges at the Tenth Annual Re-Union of the 153rd N.Y. Veteran Association, September 17, 1891. Privately printed, 1891. Montgomery County Department of History and Archives, Fonda, NY.

34. *Record of the 153rd New York State Infantry,* p. 2.

35. Harris H. Beecher, *Record of the 114th Regiment, New York State Volunteers: Where it Went, What it Saw, and What it Did,* (Norwich, NY: J.F. Hubbard, Jr., 1866), pp. 361-362.

36. *Record of the 153rd New York State Infantry,* p. 2

37. *Record of the 153rd New York State Infantry,* p.3

38. RG 94, Records of the Adjutant General's Office, 1780-1917, Compiled Military Service Record, Pvt. Lyons Wakeman, Co. H, 153rd New York Infantry, National Archives; and RG 94, Carded Medical Records, Volunteers Mexican and Civil Wars, 1846-1865, Pvt. Lyons Wakeman, Co. H, 153rd New York Infantry, National Archives.

August, 1862–June, 1863

By mid-1862, the Civil War had been underway for fourteen months. High battlefield casualties at Shiloh in the spring were a shock to the North, and high hopes for the success of Maj. Gen. George B. McClellan's Peninsular Campaign against Richmond had been crushed. Resounding military success seemed to elude Federal armies, leaving prospects for saving the Union in doubt. It was apparent that if the Rebellion was to be suppressed and the Union saved, more resources must be thrown into the fray. Thus in July, 1862 President Lincoln called on state governors to recruit 300,000 more volunteers for army service.

New York state's quota was nearly 60,000 troops, with a regiment to be raised from each senatorial district. Vigorous recruiting efforts were undertaken in most New York towns and cities, and monies were raised to offer bounties to prospective enlistees. Nineteen-year-old Sarah Rosetta Wakeman, alias Lyons Wakeman, a boatman on the Chenango Canal, was caught up in the recruitment fever when her job brought her to Montgomery County, where the 153rd Regiment, New York State Volunteers was being raised. Lyons Wakeman enrolled as a private on August 30, 1862 and mustered into service with the 153rd on October 17. Private Wakeman departed New York state with her regiment on October 18, 1862. She would never return.

Upon arrival in the nation's capital, the 153rd was assigned to the city's defenses. Stationed across the Potomac River in Alexandria, Virginia, Private Wakeman and comrades performed guard and provost marshal duty, and drilled in preparation for the day on which they would meet the enemy.

*   *   *

Alexandria
Nov. 24, 1862

My Dear Father and mother and sister and brothers, one in all,

I receive you letter on Sunday the 23. I was very glad to
hear from you and learn that you were all well. I am well and
enjoy good health. Our Regiment is in Camp at Alexandria, Va.
We have had no fighting yet. We have to guard the City and
stand on picket. I stood on my post all last night. When i left
you i went to Binghamton. I saw you there. I meet you coming
home from meeting. I went to work with Stephen Saldon the
next day. I work half a month for 4$ in money. I was only 7
miles from Binghamton up the river. I didn't go to the fair.
When i got done [with] work I went on the canal to work.[1] I
agreed to run 4 trips from Binghamton to Utica for 20$ in
money, but this load of coal was going to Canajoharie, Montgomery Co.[2]

When I got there i saw some soldiers. They wanted I should
enlist and so i did. I got 100 and 52$ in money. I enlisted for 3
years or soon [as] discharged. All the money i send you i want
you should spend it for the family in clothing or something to eat.
Don't save it for me for i can get all the money i want. If i ever
return i shall have money enough for my self and to divide with
you.

If you want to save anything to remember me by, keep that
spotted calf and if i ever return i want you to let me have her
again. Tell Robert to give her a few oats this winter and I will
pay him for doing so. Tell Celestia that I will send her my
likeness as soon as I can.[3] Mother, i will tell you where my
little Chest is. It is upstairs over the bedroom in the garret. Let
Robert go and climb up by the stove pipe hole and he will find it
on the left hand side toward the road up in the corner. I want you
should keep all my things for me for i believe that God will spare
my life and that I shall see you all again face to face before i
die.[4] Father, if you will send me some postage stamps I will be
very thankful for them. I want to drop all old affray[5] and I want
you to do the same and when i come home we will be good
friends as ever.

Good-by for the present.

Sarah Rosetta Wakeman

Direct you letter to Alexandria, Va.,
        R. L. Wakeman in the care of
        Capt. McLaughlin[6]
        Co. G, 153 Regiment, NYSV

Tell Mary i thank her for that card and I send her this little knife.[7]

Father, you needn't be a feard to write any[thing] private[8] to me for I can read all you can write. I suppose you thought that I would have to get Somebody to read it for me but I read it all my self.

                      Rosetta Wakeman

---

1. The Chenango Canal stretched 97 miles from the Susquehanna River at Binghamton in southern New York to the Erie Canal at Utica in the north of the state. Barry K. Beyer, *The Chenango Canal,* (New York: Chenango County Historical Society, 1990), p. 9.

2. Rosetta's trip extended beyond Utica, East on the Erie Canal to Canajoharie in Montgomery County, where she encountered recruiters and enrolled in the 153rd. Both Root and Fonda are in Montgomery County, NY.

3. Robert Etna Wakeman and Emily Celestia Wakeman were two of Rosetta's eight younger siblings. At the time they were 12 and 16 years old, respectively. 1860 Census, National Archives; Robert P. Wakeman, *Wakeman Genealogy, 1630-1899,* (Meriden, CT: Journal Publishing Company, 1900), p. 264.

4. Crossed out words here were "kace to kace agne be fo." Perhaps Rosetta, unused to writing, had temporarily forgotten the letter "f" and used "k" in its place, catching her mistake when she wrote "be fo." This seems likely, as she actually spelled the word "life" as "like" in the preceding sentence.

5. Spelling in the original letter is "afre." Affray is an archaic term meaning public brawl or fight.

6. Capt. George H. McLaughlin was commander of Company G, later changed to H, of the 153rd. By the end of the war he would move up the ranks to lieutenant colonel commanding the 153rd. RG 94, Compiled Military Service Record of Lt. Col. George H. McLaughlin, 153rd New York Infantry, National Archives.

7. Mary Eda Alvira Wakeman was the seventh Wakeman child and five years old at the time of Rosetta's enlistment. 1860 Census, National Archives; Robert P. Wakeman, *Wakeman Genealogy, 1630-1899,* (Meriden, CT: Journal Publishing Company, 1900), p. 264.

8. Original spelling is "prisye," which also could be privy, or private; prayers; or prosy, meaning prose.

                *   *   *

Sarah Rosetta Wakeman, alias Pvt. Lyons Wakeman,
153rd Regiment, New York State Volunteers.

Photo courtesy of Mr. Jackson K. Doane.

Capt. George H. McLaughlin, 153rd Regiment,
New York State Volunteers.

Photo courtesy of U.S. Army Military History Institute.

Alexandria, Va.
December the 23 A.D., 1862

Dear Father

I receive you letter last night. I was glad to hear from you
all. I can tell you what I done with my money if you want to
know. I got when I enlisted 100 and 52$ in money. I was
agoing to send it home but finally lent it to the first lieutenant
and sergeant. They promised to pay me when we get [a] month's
pay. We have not got it yet. They gave me their note on
interest. When I get it I will send it home to you and the family.
If you are a mind to send me a Box of apples and a Bottle of
cider, you may. The rest of the Boys are getting Boxes of stuff
from home. They get sent to them all kinds of cake and pies,
butter and cheese and bake *cicaris*. If the neighbors wants to put
something in, let them do so. You must send it by express.
Direct as you do my letters,

> R. L. Wakeman
> Alexandria, Va.
> 153 Regiment, NYSV
> Co. H, in the care of Capt. McLaughlin

I can buy anything that I want here but I have to pay double
what it is worth and I thought that I rather send home and have
you send me a Box, and when I get my pay send it home to you.
I enlisted at Montgomery County, town of Fonda [NY].
That is right, you did call that word right.
Mother and Celestia, if you will send me a pair of knit
gloves, i will thank you a thousand times. Mother, don't mourn
for me, for if I never return I hope I shall meet you all in Heaven.
I want you should forgive me of everything that I ever done, and
I will forgive you all the same.
So good-by for the present from you Affectionate Daughter,
> Rosetta Wakeman

The weather is cold and the ground is froze hard, but I sleep
as warm in the tents as I would in a good bed. I don't know the
difference when I get asleep. We have boards laid down for a
floor and our dishes is tin. We all have a tin plate and a tin cup,

and a knife and Fork, one spoon. We have to use the floor for a
table. I like to be a soldier very well.

Rosetta Wakeman

*   *   *

Alexandria, Va.
Fairfax Co.
January the 15, 1863

Dear Father,

I receive you letter today. I was much disappointed to hear
that you was not agoing to send me that box. What the express
office said to you is not so, for the Lieutenant said he did not
believe it for there is box coming in every day to someone or
nother, and I want you to send me that box, and when you put it
on the express you must make them give you a receipt for it and
send it to me in a letter, and if the Box should not come I could
go to the express office and make them pay me for it. I want you
to send me a piece of dried beef. Don't be afraid to send it for it
would kill nobody if I shouldn't get it. I Have got faith to
believe that it will come right straight through. The express
office has no business to open any box and the government is
willing that the box should be sent through to the soldiers of the
Potomac.

We have had two men die out of our Company. There has
died out of our Regiment about 30 as near as I can learn and
there is quite a number sick. We have got the measles in our
regiment.[1] There was two men taken to Washington that had
them out of the next row of tents to ourn. I Hope that God will
Suffer me not to get them again.[2] For your sake I have got faith
to believe that I shall come home once more before I die, but if it
is God will for me to die here it is my will to die here, his will be
done instead of ours on earth as in heaven. I feel to put my
whole hope and trust in Him. He is all that I have to look to
when I am in trouble. I hope that if I never meet you again on
earth that I shall meet you all in Heaven.

I will see the Captain about them papers and if he will make
them out for me I will send them right to you, and then you can
go to the town of Afton and get you money. If I do get the papers
and you get the money, I want you to divide it with the family

and get them some Clothes with the money. I will get it all to
you.

I receive the glove and the mittens, yarn, needle and cans. I
was very thankful for them. Mother, I will send you and Celestia
some money when I draw my pay. Father, don't worry about the
money that I lent for I shall get the most of it, and if I don't I
shall gain it again. The boys that I lent it to live a good ways
from you and it is not worth you trouble. They live way up
North and I will look out for my Self. I was foolish in lend[ing]
it. But if I ever get it again I will send it home to the family.

Don't be afraid to send the box for I Shall get it. I want you
to Write soon as you get this. So good-by for the present from
you Affectionate,

Rosetta Wakeman

Direct you letter as you did before and the box as you did
the letters. I don't see anything more to write at present.

Rosetta Wakeman

Mother, I use all of the tobacco I want. I think it will keep
off from catch[ing] diseases. I wish you all well and I hope that
I shall meet you all again, so goodby for the present from you
Affectionate,   Sarah Rosetta Wakeman

I would like some postage stamps for it is hard work to get
them. When I draw my pay I will send you all some money and
my likeness in two separate cases. Today is my birthday for it is
the 16th of January. I wrote part of this letter yester[day] on the
15th.

I send my respects to you all. Tell Frank[3] that I want him to
Write to me, for I have not receive only one letter from him.
Good-by for the present from your Affectionate,

Rosetta Wakeman

---

1. Here "smallpox" is crossed out and measles is written above.
2. Medical records reveal that Pvt. Wakeman was admitted to the
Regimental Hospital on January 1, 1863 with a diagnosis of "Rubeola,"
and released January 7. In December, 1862, the 153rd's colonel ordered
the vaccination of the entire command for smallpox, so it is possible that
Rosetta was suffering from a mild case of smallpox due to the crude
vaccination practices of the day. RG 94, Carded Medical Records,
Volunteers, Mexican and Civil Wars, 1846-1865, National Archives;

RG 94, Regimental Order Book, 153rd New York Infantry, National Archives.

3. Frank R. Roberts was Rosetta's cousin (See pages 51-2 and 56 for his letters to the Wakeman family).

*   *   *

Alexandria Va.
February the 20, 1863

Mother,

I send 4 dollars. I want you [to] let Robert have 1 and Celestia 1, Lois 1,[1] and keep the other you self. Robert, you let Father take the money and buy you a knife for to remember me by.

I am well at present and I hope those lines will find you all the same.

Rosetta Wakeman
R. L. Wakeman

Give this ring to susan.[2]

---

1. Lois Amelia Wakeman, third child of the Wakeman family and 13 years old when this letter was written. 1860 U.S. Census, National Archives; Wakeman, *Wakeman Genealogy*, p. 263-264.

2. Susan Althea Wakeman was the fifth Wakeman child and was nine years old. 1860 U.S. Census, National Archives; Wakeman, pp. 263-264.

*   *   *

Alexandria Va.
Fairfax Co.
March the 29/63

excitement of war

Dear Father,

    I take my time to write a few lines to you and let you know
that I am well. I receive a letter from you today. I was much
pleased with it. I am sorry to learn that you did not get that
money from the town of Afton. I will see the Captain and get
him to make out some more papers and I will send them to you. I
have got part of that money I lent but I have spent it and I shall
get the rest. We expect to get four months pay this week and if I
do I shall have 60 dollars in money. I am getting 13 dollars per
month. I will send part of it home to you. The smallpox has
cease. I have not heard anything about it in some time.
    You mustn't trouble you Self about me. I am contented. I
want you to get along the best way you can until this war is over.
I believe that God will spare my life to come home once more.
Then I will help you to pay you debts. I will send you more or
less money while I am a soldier. When I get out of the service I
will make money enough to pay all the debts that you owe.
    I sent that likeness by express and paid the freight. It was
mark Harpersville, Broome Co., N.Y., Harvey Wakeman.[1] I
will have my likeness taken again and send it to you all.
    Our regiment don't expect to stay here long. I don't know
where we shall go to. Some think that we shall go into a Fort
into heavy artillery. For my part I don't care where we go to. I
don't fear the rebel bullets nor I don't fear the cannon. I have
heard the heavy roar of the cannon. I have to go on guard every
other day and drill the day that I am not on guard. I like to drill
first rate. We have battalion drill every afternoon at 2 o'clock
and drill till 4 o'clock. We load and fire our guns on drill. We
fire blank cartridge. Our major that drill us was a captain in one
of the N.Y. regiment.[2] He was in the 7 days fight before Richmond. He is a smart little fellow.
    Good-by for this time. You Affectionate,
                R. L. Wakeman

    When you think of me think where I am. It would make
your hair stand out to be where I have been. How would you

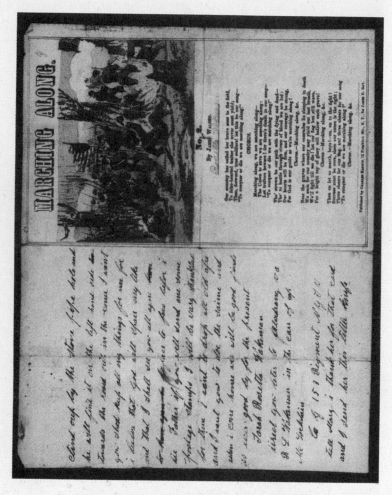

Detail from November 24, 1862 letter. Note the
signature line and directions for return mail at left.

Photo courtesy of Mr. Jackson K. Doane.

like to be in the front rank and have the rear rank load and fire
their guns over you shoulder? I have been there my Self.

I am getting fat as a hog. The climate agrees with me first
rate. I am the fattest[3] fellow you ever see. Write to me soon as
you get this letter. I send my love to you all, this from you
Affectionate,

Rosetta Wakeman

I have had a letter from Sarah Wheeler and I have wrote her
one. Tell Lois that I thank her for them postage stamps.

Father, I send you that receipt I got to the express office for
that likeness.

---

1. The Harvey Wakeman homestead was probably closer to
Harpersville, in Broome County, NY, than to the town of Afton, NY.

2. Maj. Edwin P. Davis, who would be promoted to colonel
commanding the 153rd on May 1, 1863. Prior to accepting his commis-
sion in the 153rd, Davis served as a lieutenant and captain in the 62nd
NYSV, which saw action during the Seven Days in McClellan's 1862
Peninsular Campaign. RG 94, Compiled Military Service Record, Col.
Edwin P. Davis, 153rd New York Infantry, National Archives; RG 15,
Pension Record SC 153.669, Col. and Bvt. Brig. Gen. Edwin P. Davis,
National Archives; Frederick H. Dyer, *A Compendium of the War of the
Rebellion*, (New York, NY: Thomas Yoseloff, [1908] 1959), p. 191.

3. The original spelling is "fa laest." The "l" is interpreted here as
an uncrossed "t." Scratched in the end of "laest" is "est."

* * *

Alexandria Va.
Fairfax Co.
April the 13, 1863

Dear Father and Mother, Brother and Sister,

It is with pleasure that I Write a few lines to you and let you
know that I am well at present and I hope these lines will find
you all the same.

Our regiment has exchanged guns. We have got enfield
Rifle. We have got Marching orders. We expect to March
tomorrow at one o'clock. We have got three days rations cook
all ready for us. I don't know where we Shall go. You needn't
write to me until I write to [you] again.

I feel perfectly happy. If I go into a battle I shall be alright. It is what I have wish for a good while. I hope that God will Spare my life. I believe He will. I don't dread it at all. Don't forget to pray for me. There has not a day pass since I left you but I have thought of home and have had appeal[1] with God. Let God will be done on earth as in heaven. If it is God will for me to be killed here, it is my will to die.

So good-by for this time. This is from you affectionate,

Rosetta Wakeman

Give those verses to Mother.

---

1. Original is "a pear." Other possible interpretations are "a peace" or "a piece," referring to a conversation with God.

*   *   *

Alexandria, Va.
April the 30/63

Dear Father and Mother,

I take my time to Write to you. I am well at present and enjoying myself first rate. We have got four months Pay. I will send you 30$ as soon as I can get to the express office. I wrote to you some time ago for we got marching Orders but we have not march yet and I don't know when we shall. I want you all to write to me Just the same as you did before. Direct you letters to Alexandria, Va.

Rosetta Wakeman

Celestia, I want you and Lois to send me you likeness. Send it [to] me in a letter Just the same as i sent this to you.

Celestia, I send you my likeness in this letter. It cost me 50 cents. I will have my likeness taken again in another form and send it [to] Lois in my next letter. Write to me as soon as you get this letter. This is from you Affectionate Sister,

Sarah Rosetta Wakeman

I have found some names in the Burying Ground here that is of some importance. They are Soldiers that are buried here.

The first is. John. More Co. F. 21. NY regiment. I think it is Ida Smith Brother. I want you to find out and let me know.

The next is Wimbur. Smith. Co. H. 46. NY. I think he is John Smith Brother.

Henry O. Sanders. Co. i. 5. Wisconsin.[1]

john. Cot. Co. H. 36. NY regiment.

---

1. Henry Sanders of Emerson's Co., 5th Wisconsin Infantry, died of chronic diarrhea on November 2, 1862, and was buried in grave number 419, Military Cemetery, Alexandria, Va. RG 94, Compiled Military Service Record, Pvt. Henry O. Saunders, Co. I, 5th Wisconsin Volunteer Infantry, National Archives.

*   *   *

Alexandria Va.
May the 25, 1863

Dear Sister Phronia,[1]

I once more thought of [letter torn]. I am well and I [letter torn] those lines will find you the same. I have not sent you anything yet. I have sent all of the rest something. Now I send you this little Book to remember me. Our Chaplain[2] gave it to me yesterday and I thought I would send it [to] you.

                    Rosetta Wakeman

Mary, I send this Card to you I often think of you. I remember well the last time I ever saw you then [letter torn] I kiss you and bid you good-by. Ros [letter torn].

Lois, I want you to Write to me as soon as you can. I forgive you of every thing that you ever done to me and I want you to do the same. So good-by for this time.

                    Rosetta Wakeman

---

1. Sophronia Angelia was the sixth Wakeman child and nine years old. 1860 U.S. Census, National Archives; Wakeman, p. 263.

2. Chaplain Jacob H. Enders, 153rd New York State Volunteers, commissioned in 1862 and mustered out with the regiment in 1865. Rev. Jacob H. Enders, *Letters, 1862-1881*. Montgomery County Department of History and Archives, Fonda, NY.

*   *   *

City of Alexandria, Virginia, with Fort Ellsworth on hill in the distance.
Photo courtesy of National Archives.

Alexandria Provost Marshal's Office.
Matthew Brady photo, courtesy of National Archives.

Alexandria Va.
May the 30/63

Dear Mother,

It is with pleasure that I Write to you. I receive a letter from you all the other day. I was down to the Provost Marshal on Patrol in the City. That is the same as a Policeman in the City. I am well at Present. I am glad to learn that you have got that money. I give it to you all. Do what you are a mind to with it.

I can't think of anything more to Write at Present. Write soon.

Rosetta Wakeman

*   *   *

Alexandria Va.
June the 5, 1863

Dear Parents,

It is with Affectionate love that I Write to you and let you know that I am well at Present and enjoying myself the best I can. I am glad that you did not let Rolf have any of that money I sent to you. When I send you money I want you to lay it out for the family.

I can tell you what made me leave home. It was because I had got tired of stay[ing] in that neighborhood. I knew that I Could help you more to leave home than to stay there with you. So I left. I am not sorry that I left you. I believe that it will be all for the best yet. I believe that God will spare my life to come home once more. When I get out of this war I will come home and see you but I Shall not stay long before I shall be off to take care of my Self. I will help you all I can as long as I live.

If I ever own a farm It will be in Wisconsin. On the Prairie.[1] I [am] enjoying my Self better this summer than I ever did before in this world. I have good Clothing and enough to eat and nothing to do, only to handle my gun and that I can do as well as the rest of them.

I don't want you to mourn about me for I can take care of my Self and I know my business as well as other folks know them for me. I will Dress as I am a mind to for all anyone else [cares], and if they don't let me Alone they will be sorry for it.

Write to me all about Alfonzo.[2] Tell him that I can make the best soldier than he would. I can't think of anything more to Write, so good-by for this time.

Rosetta Wakeman

As I set here aWrite I can hear the Cannon Roar from Fort Lyon. Fort Lyon is on one side of us and Fort Ellsworth on the other side.[3]

Rosetta Wakeman

---

1. Original is *Parers*.

2. Alfonzo Stewart is listed on the 1850 Census as living with the Wakeman family. He was reported to be 32 years of age, making him approximately 45 at the time Rosetta wrote this letter. The Census reports "none" for Stewart's occupation. 1850 U.S. Census, National Archives.

3. Fort Ellsworth was located directly west of Alexandria near where the Masonic Monument stands today. Fort Lyon was located directly south of Fort Ellsworth on the Telegraph Road, below Hunting Creek. Benjamin F. Cooling and Walton H. Owen, *Mr. Lincoln's Forts,* (Shippensburg, PA: White Mane Publishing Co., 1988), pp. 39-40, 60-64. These were just two of the 118 forts and batteries constituting the defenses of Washington in 1863, complemented by 20,000 to 50,000 troops. Benjamin F. Cooling, *Symbol Sword & Shield: Defending Washington During the Civil War,* (Shippensburg, PA: White Mane Publishing Co., second revised edition, 1991), pp. 149-153.

*   *   *

Alexandria Va.
June the 19, A.D. 1863

Dear Mother,

I take my time to Write to you and let you [know] that I am well. I haven't had a letter from home in some time.

Our regiment got two month's pay the 9th of June. I sent 10$ dollars to father, one locket to you, one necktie to Robert. I sent it by express and paid the fare. You will find it to Deposit. I Direct it to Deposit, Del. Co. NY, NY and Erie RR.

I want you to Write soon as you get this letter. This sheet of paper cost me 5 cents in money.

Rosetta Wakeman

I sent Lois my likeness in a letter the other day. Father I want you to Write, too, and let me know all about you Farming and how long do you intend to keep Fony?[1] What day of the month did he come back to live with you again and what made him go off last Fall? Please tell me all about it.

What do you think of this war? I think I shall have to stay my three years in the army. I can't think of any thing more to Write.

Rosetta Wakeman

---

1. "Fony" and "Fon" are probably nicknames for Alfonzo Stewart.

* * *

July, 1863–December, 1863

Over two years of war had passed and the outlook for ultimate defeat of Southern armies was still dim. Union military victories were few, and each battle seemed more grim and costly than the last. But resolve in the North had hardened. No cost in human life was too dear to reunify the country and to accomplish a new purpose, the freeing of millions of enslaved African Americans. President Lincoln called for 300,000 more volunteers, and when recruiting became more difficult, a draft was imposed in July, 1863. The Emancipation Proclamation, in effect since January, represented a shift in the North's war aims and made possible a new resource of fighting men. By mid-1863 the War Department was actively involved in recruiting U.S. Colored Troops, who would eventually number 178,975. Over two million U.S. soldiers, sailors, and marines would serve by the war's end.

Union victory at Gettysburg on July 3 signaled a change in the war fortunes of the U.S. Government. It was followed by a more decisive victory when Vicksburg on the Mississippi River fell into Federal hands on July 4. The government's fear for the safety of Washington City, however, kept thousands of troops, including the 153rd New York State Volunteers, within the capital's defenses for the remainder of the year.

*   *   *

Alexandria, Va.
July 2, 1863

excitement

Dear Father,

  I receive you letter today. I was glad to hear from you once
more. I am well at present and I hope these lines will find you
all the Same.
  Our regiment lays here yet and I don't know how long we
shall stay here. The rebs is amaking Such work in Maryland and
Pennsylvania that I don't know how long before we shall be call
on for a reinforcement.[1] For my part I am ready at a minute's
warning to go into the field of battle and take my stand with the
rest. They are ablockading this City of Alexandria very strong
for they expect Attack here. Our regiment has laid out in the
field for some time every night, awatching for the rebels. I am in
hopes that they will come, for if they do they will get lick. There
is three regiment of infantry here and one of Cavalry and some
flying artillery.
  Write to me soon as you get this letter. This from you
Affectionate,

                              Rosetta Wakeman

---

  1. The Battle of Gettysburg was fought July 1-3, 1863 in southern
Pennsylvania, approximately 70 miles from Washington, D.C.

                *   *   *

Alexandria, Va.
[no date]

Father,

  What do you think about that draft in [New] york State? Do
you think that you will be drafted or not? I would like to know
in you next letter. Write all about it to me and how you feel
about it. If you are drafted I want you to come into my regiment
and my Co. if you Can.
  I Suppose you know all about that fuss in [New] york City
about that draft. I hope that the Governor of [New] york State

will put it down and the draft will go on.[1] I would like to see some of them Copperheads Come down here and get killed. It would do me good to see it done.

I Can't think of anything more to Write at Present, so good-by for this time. This is from you Affectionate,

Rosetta Wakeman

I receive two postage stamps in that letter. I was glad to get them. I would be very thankful to you if you would send me some postage stamps When you Write to me for I Can't get them every day here.

Rosetta Wakeman

---

1. A reference to the New York City Draft Riots, which occurred July 14-15, 1863.

*   *   *

[No place or date]

For my part I think that I shall have to stay my three years in the army if I don't get killed or discharge. For the way this war is carried on, if they would knock down the officers' pay to 13$ a month this war would soon be settle, for all they are afighting for is their pay, and as long as they Can they will Keep it agoing. When one officer gets all the money he wants, he will resign his office, then someone else will take his place.

If I ever get Clear from the army I will come home and make you a visit, but I shall not stay long for I can content my self somewhere else in this world. For my part I never shall live in that neighborhood again.

The weather is very warm here. How do you like the looks of my likeness? Do you think I look better than I did when I was to home? I would like to have you send me Robert's likeness if you can.

Rosetta Wakeman

*   *   *

HeadQuarters,[1]
Department of Washington
July 20, 1863

Special Order   }
No. 139   }
[Extract]

   5. *The 153rd Regiment, New York Volunteers, Col. E.
P. Davis [commanding], is hereby relieved from duty with
Brig. Genl. J.P. Slough [in Alexandria] and will report to Brig.
General J.H. Martindale, Military Governor, District of
Columbia, for duty in the City Washington.*
   *The Regiment will march immediately on receipt of
this order. The camp baggage and garrison equipage will
follow.*

                    By command of
                    Major Genl. [Samuel] Heintzelman

---

   1. RG 94, Regimental Order Book, 153rd New York Infantry,
National Archives. This order for transfer to Washington was issued to
the 153rd in preparation for expected draft riots in Washington similar to
those that occurred in New York City. *Record of the 153rd New York
State Infantry,* read by Lt. George H. Hodges at the Tenth Annual Re-
Union of the 153rd N.Y. Veteran Association, September 17, 1891.
Montgomery County Department of History and Archives, Fonda, NY.

                 *   *   *

Washington, D.C.
July the 27, 1863

Dear Mother,

   I take my time to Write to you and let you [know] that I am
well and I hope these lines will find you the same. I have wrote
several letters to you all since I have had any letters from home.
   Our regiment has left Alexandria, Va. and gone to Washington. Our regiment is in Barrack. We have got good quarters.
Our regiment is next to regulars. Colonel Edwin Davis is so
strict with the men that we don't like to stay here. We had

Maj. Edwin P. Davis, 153rd Regiment, New York State Volunteers.
Promoted to colonel and took command of the 153rd on May 1, 1863.

Photo courtesy of National Archives.

Officers of the 153rd Regiment, New York State Volunteers in camp.

Photo courtesy of U.S. Army Military History Institute, Carlisle Barracks.

drother go to the front. Our regiment has got a good Brass Band to play for us when we mount guard.

I am in hopes that this war will soon be over so that I Can Come home once more in this World. Write soon as you get this letter and let me know if you have sent Robert likeness or not and where it was Direct. I send you one dollar in this to you to buy snuff with. I use a good deal of tobacco. I have what money I ought to use and Send some home to you, but I spend more money here than I would if I was to home. I have sent 60 dollars in money home but there was 5 dollars that you never got. I have sent 55 dollars that you have got and if I live I will send all the money I Can spare. So good-by for this time.

So you Can see, that I think as much of you and the rest of the family as I ever did, and if I ever live to Come home I will do as much for you as I ever did. Write soon as you get this letter and let me know all about What is agoing on there. Please let me know. So good-by for this time. Direct you letter to Washington, D.C.

Rosetta Wakeman

Give this 25 cents to Robert.

Rosetta Wakeman

*   *   *

[No place or date]

Dear Father,

I will Write a few lines to you and let you know What kind of quarters we have got. We are in Barrack. They are good ones.

My Co. and Co. C is in one building. The buildings is two story high. The place for to sleep is upstairs and down below is a room for to do the Cooking and a place to eat. We can get good Water to drink outside of the guard. It is Well Water. We Can get Water to Wash With inside of the guard. It is Water that comes from the river. This river Water is a little salty, for the tide *sit* up the river as far as George town.

I can't think of any more to write at Present so good-by.

Direct you letter to   Washington, D.C.
                          153 NYSV Co. H
                          in care of Capt. McLaughlin

                          Rosetta Wakeman

                    *   *   *

Capitol Hill
Washington D.C.
August the 5, A.D. 1863

My Dear Father and Mother,

   I take my time to Write a few lines to you and let you know
that I am well. I hope those lines will find you all the same. I
got a letter from you today. I was glad to hear from home once
more. I got a letter from home the other day and got 8 postage
stamps in it. I was glad to get them. I will thank you a thousand
times for them. I will ask you one question and I would like to
have you answer it. Did you peel that hemlock that blowed
down in the sugar place? Have you peel them hemlock that are
over 'cross the Brook? What size is that hay barn that you built
this summer up on the hill? If you please, let me know in you
next letter.
       I don't know how long our regiment will stay here. When
we leave i will sit down and Write a letter to you and let you
know all about it. We expect some drafted men to fill up our
regiment. They have drafted a good many men in Washington.
They have drafted black men as well as White men.[1] They are
adrafting every day here now.
      It is a very pretty place here. Where our barrack is the road
runs all around our Camp grounds. There are some pretty houses
here. We are Right in sight of the united states Capitol. It is one
hundred feet high from the ground to the top of it and there is
men to work on it all of the time.[2] This building is made all of
marble stones. I have been inside of it. I have been in the
Congress hall. That is a pretty place you better believe.
      Our regiment has sent some of our men to the invalid Corps
today. The one that went out of our Co. today is Gilbert War-

ren.[3] That is his name. We have got a good many men in the hospital now. There was one man died yesterday in the hospital. He belong to Co. C.

Rosetta Wakeman

I don't know how long before i shall have to go into the field of battle. For my part i don't Care. I don't feel afraid to go. I don't believe there are any Rebel's bullet made for me yet. Nor i don't Care if there is. I am as independent as a hog on the ice. If it is God will for me to fall in the field of battle, it is my will to go and never return home.

Write as soon as you get this letter. So good-by for this time, from yours respectful,

Miss Rosetta Wakeman
Rosetta Wakeman

---

1. U.S. Government efforts to recruit black troops were well underway by mid-1863, coordinated by the Bureau of Colored Troops in the War Department. Dudley Taylor Cornish, *The Sable Arm: Black Troops in the Union Army, 1861-1865*, (University Press of Kansas, [1956] 1987), pp. 110-130, 129-131; James M. McPherson, *The Negro in the Civil War*, (New York: Vintage Books, 1965), pp. 161-182.

2. Although occupied by Congress, the dome of the U.S. Capitol Building was still under construction at this time.

3. Pvt. Gilbert Warren was ordered to the Invalid Corps on August 6, 1863. His disability is recorded as varicocele, a tumor formed in the varicose veins. RG 94, Compiled Military Service Record of Gilbert Warren, Co. H, 153rd New York Infantry, National Archives.

*   *   *

Capitol Hill
Washington, D.C.
August the 19/63

Dear Parents,

It is with affectionate love that I take my time to Write to you and let you know that I am well and I hope those lines will find you all the same. I receive you letter today and I was glad to hear from home once more.

I stand guard every other day at the Prison, Where there is some Rebels Prisoner and some Rebels officers.[1] They are smart looking men. They say that they wish this war was over so that they Could go home but I don't believe that this war will be over as long as there is a man left, and for my part I don't Care how long it does last. I hope that our regiment will have to go into the field before it is over. Then I shall be satisfied and not until we have to go.

I Can get all kinds of fruit here that I want, but I have to pay a good price for it. I Can get Watermelon, muskmelon, peaches, pears, apples, figs, raisins, and grain Corn and all kinds of grain stuff.[2] If you will send me some more postage stamps i will be very thankful for them.

If Frank have to go to the army, tell him that he must Write to me and I will write to him. If you can find out what regiment Henry Austin is in and what Co., I Would like to know and where his regiment is alaying.[3] I Can't think of anything more to Write at Present, so good-by for this time from yours truly,

Miss Rosetta Wakeman

The Weather is very warm here and it is Cold nights. *The Citizen* says that it has been the hottest Weather this summer that has been before in ten years. Write soon as you get this letter.

Rosetta Wakeman

---

1. Carroll Prison was located on Capitol Hill near First and A Streets, where the Old Capitol Prison stood. James Joseph Williamson, *Prison Life in the Old Capitol and Reminiscences of the Civil War,* (West Orange, NJ: N.p., 1911), pp. 20-22. Rosetta Wakeman appears on the Carroll Prison Guard Reports during August, September, and October of 1863. She is listed variously as "L. Wakeman," "R.L. Wakeman," and "R. Wakeman." Record Group 393, Records of U.S. Army Continental Commands, Vol. 329, A[DW]12, Carroll Prison Guard Reports, National Archives. See p. 45 for detail of September 14, 1863 Guard Report.

2. Rosetta's spelling of "grain" is "greain," which could also be interpreted as "green corn" and "green stuff."

3. Frank Roberts, Rosetta's cousin. Henry Austin was a friend of Rosetta's from home who enlisted in the 109th New York.

*   *   *

[No place or date]

I have just thought of something new to Write to you. It is as following.

Over to Carroll Prison they have got three women that is Confined in their Rooms. One of them was a Major in the union army and she went into battle with her men. When the Rebels bullets was acoming like a hail storm she rode her horse and gave orders to the men. Now She is in Prison for not doing aCcordingly to the regulation of war.

The other two is rebel Spies and they have Catch them and Put them in Prison. They are Smart looking women and [have] good education.[1]

I Can't think of any more to Write at this time. Write soon as you get this letter.

Rosetta Wakeman

---

1. Prisoner and other records available for Carroll Prison are incomplete, so the identity of the Union woman major remains a mystery. The two women Rebel spies, however, were probably Belle Boyd and her roommate. Boyd was famous for her spying exploits for Maj. Gen. T.J. "Stonewall" Jackson during his 1862 Shenandoah Valley Campaign. Boyd was an inmate of Carroll Prison from August through December, 1863, her second term of imprisonment in Washington. Her roommate in Carroll Prison for a portion of this time was Ida P., who was arrested by Federal authorities on a charge of being a Rebel mail carrier. August, 1863 diary entry from Belle Boyd, *In Camp and Prison,* (London: Saunders, Otley & Company, 1865), in Katherine M. Jones, *Heroines of Dixie,* (New York: Bobbs-Merrill, 1955), pp. 254-258.

*　　　*　　　*

Capitol Hill
Washington, D.C.
September the 3/63

Dear Father, Mother, Brothers and Sister,

I take my time today to Write a few lines to you all. I receive you letter yesterday. I was glad to hear from you once more. I am well at present and I hope those few lines will find you all the same.

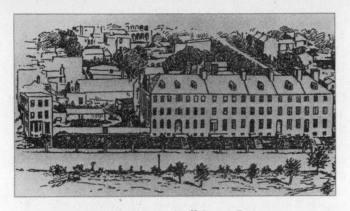

Carroll Prison, or Duff Green's Row.
From Prison Life in the Old Capitol and Reminiscences of the Civil War, *1911.*

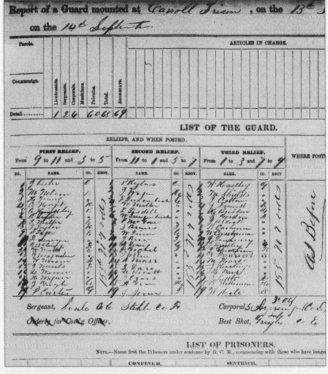

Detail from September 14, 1863 Carroll Prison
Guard Report. Rosetta Wakeman is listed as No. 18 on the third relief.
Photo courtesy of National Archives.

I was on Camp guard yesterday and got relieve this morning at nine O'Clock. Our regiment have to guard five different places. One is Camp guard, Second is Carroll prison, third is Depot guard, fourth is City hall, and the fifth is City guard. They go out every night and Come back in the morning. The City Hall guard goes out in the morning and Come back at night. The City Hall guard is where the draft is Carried on here. There they exam[ine] the men there and Some of them get exempt. They have drafted black men as well as White men. When the men is passed into the army, they are taken off by a guard to the place of rendezvous.

There is nothing new going on here. I Can't think of any more to Write at present So good-by. Please Write to me all About Frank and Dewit Wakeman,[1] also Henry Austin. When you get another paper from Uncle Robert I would like to have you send me one of them papers.

If you Can read this letter you will do better than I think you Can. I Can read all of you writing. From yours far and distant friend,

Rosetta Wakeman

I received three postage stamps in you letter. I Was glad for I hadn't got none.

Rosetta Wakeman

---

1. DeWitt Wakeman was Rosetta's 22-year-old cousin, son of her Uncle John Wakeman of Harpersville, New York. Wakeman, p. 262.

*　　　*　　　*

Capitol Hill
Washington, D.C.
September the 20/63

Dear Father,

I take this present time to Write a few lines to you and Mother. Today is Sunday and I have nothing to hinder my writing to you. I have not wrote in some time to you, nor I haven't had a letter from home in a good while. You must excuse me for not Write any sooner to you. I am well and enjoy myself first rate for a soldier.

I think I like this place better than I did Alexandria for our guard duty is all in [the] same building. Our regiment has to guard Carroll Prison and the Depot and City hall. When I am down to the Depot and see so many men and women agoing North it makes me homesick. There is some of our men that have got a furlough and gone home. John Webb has got one and he is agoing to start tonight for home to greenfield Center, Saratoga Co., but I don't think that it would be my luck to get a furlough to come home this fall.[1] For my part I shan't try for it. If I did the officers Would say, "No, you must let the married men go home first." You must live in hope for I have been gone one year and I have only two years [yet] to stay in the army.

When you Write to me again I want to know where Frank is and where he had to go, to the army or not, and if you Can find out what Company Henry Austin is in and Where to Direct a letter to him. I have been gone one year and I haven't Seen a man nor a woman that I ever seen before I left home. I have been along with entire strangers to me. Don't you think that I have Stood it well? I haven't been sick but once and that was last Winter when I had the measles.

We have got a pretty Brass band in our regiment. The musicians is pretty good at it.[2] Our old bugler is as big as Uncle John Wakeman.

I want to know how you got along with you interest[s] this fall and how much Stock you are agoing to winter, and is Fon agoing to stay with you this Winter or not? I want to know. So good-by this time.

Rosetta Wakeman

---

1. On the January, 1864 returns, John Webb is listed as a deserter, having gone home to Greenfield, Saratoga Co., NY on furlough and never returning. He returned voluntarily on February 1, 1864, and later died of chronic diarrhea in a New Orleans hospital in June. RG 94, Compiled Military Service Record, Pvt. John Webb, Co. H, 153rd New York Infantry, National Archives.

2. The 153rd Regiment's brass band was good enough to be ordered to play at a White House function in February, 1864. RG 94, Regimental Order Book, 153rd New York Infantry, National Archives.

*   *   *

Capitol Hill
Washington, D.C.
October the 9, 1863

Dear Father and mother,

I take my time to write a letter to you this evening. I receive a letter from you yesterday. I was glad to hear from you once more. I am well and as tough as a bear. This Southern climate agrees with me first rate and I hope it will agree with Frank. I am Sorry to learn that Frank is where he is but it Can't be help now.[1] Tell aunt Susan that she mustn't feel too bad about Frank for I have been enlisted one year and haven't Seen but one dead person since I have been in the army. I wrote Frank a letter yesterday.

We are adrilling nowadays. Company drill in the morning and a battalion drill in the afternoon. For my part I like to drill. I think a Skirmish[2] drill is the prettiest drill that ever was drill. I have got So that I Can drill just as well as any man there is in my regiment. When Colonel Davis gives a order I know What the regiment is agoing to do just as well as he does. We was on a battalion drill the other day and we was aCharging 'bout and agoing double quick and one of Co. C men felled down and got the bayonet run through his leg. You better believe that he bled like a Stuck hog.

Dear Mother,

It Seem like a dream to me to think of home, although I realize that there is Such a place in this world. Mr. Hiram Sweet got a telegraph dispatch the other day that his Son Robert was dead, and what do you Suppose that he did to keep from feeling bad about it?[3] He got drunk and hasn't drawed a Sober breath since. I suppose you think that is [a] rather hard life to live, but it is nothing but what Some of them does in the army. I can't think of any more to write at present, so good by from,

Rosetta Wakeman

How do you like the looks of my envelope that is printed on the directions?[4]

Rosetta Wakeman

1. Frank R. Roberts, Rosetta's cousin, was drafted on July 17, 1863, for service in the 64th New York State Volunteers. He was reported sick in the U.S. Army General Hospital at Fairfax Seminary for September through November, 1863. RG 94, Compiled Military Service Record, Pvt. Frank R. Roberts, 64th New York Infantry, National Archives.

2. Rosetta's original spelling of this word is "Curish." An infantry training manual used by Federal forces from 1862 through the end of the war yields "skirmish" drill as the closest match for "Curish." Brig. Gen. Silas Casey, *Infantry Tactics, for the Instruction, Exercise, and Manoeuvres of The Soldier, A Company, Line of Skirmishers, Battalion, Brigade, of Corps D'Armee,* (Dayton, OH: Morningside House, Inc., [1862]1985), pp. 181-223.

3. In Pvt. Hiram Sweet's military records is a letter dated September 29, 1863, certifying that his son, Robert, is dangerously ill with typhoid fever, and desires to see his father, who is in the 153rd New York State Volunteers. Pvt. Hiram Sweet died of fever on April 24, 1864, at Alexandria, LA. RG 94, Compiled Military Service Record, Pvt. Hiram Sweet, Co. G, 153rd New York Infantry, National Archives.

4. Photo of several of Rosetta's envelopes appears on page 50. The addresses on several envelopes appear to have been typeset.

*   *   *

Capitol Hill
Washington, D.C.
October the 13, 1863

Dear Father and Mother,

I take this present time to Write a few lines to you and let you know that I am well and I hope those few lines will find you the Same.

The 109 N.Y. regiment is at Georgetown, D.C. They went there yesterday. I Saw them when they left the Depot. I Stood on the platform to the Depot when they started for Georgetown and as quick as I found out that they was 109 N.Y. I could hardly Stand it. I was on provost guard in the City so that I Couldn't See Henry Austin but as Soon as I got to Camp I went to my lieutenant and got a pass for today and this morning I Started for Georgetown, and when I got there they was on an island in the River. I got a man to row me across the River to the island and then I found Henry Austin and Perry Wilder.[1] They knew me just as Soon as they see me. You better believe I had a good visit with them. I stayed about two Hours and Started back for Camp again. I got back about two O'Clock in the afternoon.[2]

Several of Rosetta Wakeman's envelopes. Note Alexandria,
Washington, D.C., and New Orleans postmarks.

Photo courtesy of Mr. Jackson K. Doane.

Our regiment expect to move before long. Where we Shall go I don't know, nor I don't Care. For my part I hope we Shall go to South Carolina, for there is nothing so lovely as the Southern Sun. When it rises over the virginia hills and Shines into the vales of South Carolina, I then like to be a Soldier. The hotter the Sun Shines, the better I like it in the army.

I can't think of any more to Write at present. So good-by for the present.

from Rosetta Wakeman

---

1. Sgt. William Henry Austin and Pvt. Perry Albert Wilder served in the 109th New York State Volunteers, which was transferred to the 22nd Army Corps in Washington for railroad guard in 1863. RG 94, Compiled Military Service Records, Sgt. William Henry Austin and Pvt. Perry Albert Wilder, Co. D, 109th New York Infantry, National Archives; Frederick H. Dyer, *A Compendium of the War of Rebellion,* Vol. II (New York: Thomas Yoseloff, Publisher, [1908] 1959), p. 1448.

Perry Wilder was also a second cousin of Rosetta's. Burl A. Wilder, *Wilder Genealogy,* courtesy of Mrs. Ruth Goodier, Chipley, Florida. After the war, Perry Wilder's younger brother, Alva Wells (Jack) Wilder, married one of Rosetta's sisters, Susan Althea. After Susan's death, he married Sophronia, another of Rosetta's sisters, in 1885. Wakeman, p. 264.

2. This visit to the 109th New York at what is now named Roosevelt Island raises an interesting point, in that Rosetta probably visited her friends from home while attired in uniform. Thus Austin and Wilder were two more people added to a widening circle of family and friends who knew that she was serving in the army under an assumed male identity.

*   *   *

[*The following was found among Rosetta's letters and is from Frank R. Roberts to the Wakeman family.*]

Oct. 27, 1863
Fairfax Seminary, Ward B
near Alexandria, Va.

Dear Uncle, Aunt & Cousins,

I now take the opportunity to inform you that I received your letter yesterday of the fourth in reply to mine. I was very glad to hear from you and to hear that you was all well.

I am gaining very fast now. I have got quite smart so that I walk out a considerable [while]. You need not answer this until you hear from me again because I expect that we are agoing to move. They say that they are agoing to take us to our own state hospital. If so I probably shall soon be in the hospital at New York city. Just as soon as I get to a stop I will write to you again.

The Ohio boys started yesterday for their state hospital but they got back last night. We asked them what the war news was in Ohio and how the corn crop was this year. They allowed that their travel was mostly in the night and they could not see. They finally allowed that it was a military move and let it go at that.

You wanted me to write whether there was anybody in my regiment that I knew before that I left home. I am happy to say that there is Asa L. Austin, Philip Austin, Warren B. Parsons.[1] He is Chas. Parson's son. They was with me all the time from the time that I left home 'til I came away from my regiment. When I got here I found Henry Scouten, Gill Conroe and Frank Knapp. They are from Cold Spring Brook, Delaware county.

I received six letters yesterday. They had been to the regiment and just got back. One was from Edwin R. Wakeman, Capitol Hill, Washington, D.C.[2] I answered that last night. Tell Lois that I will answer her letter before many days. I get letters from home quite often now. It was six weeks from the time I came from home 'til I got a letter. I wrote to you three or four days ago so I have no news to write.

Father went away from here this morning. He came here Friday. He found me much better than he expected. My love & good wishes to all. Good-by,

Frank R. Roberts

---

1. Warren B. Parsons, Philip N. Austin, and Asa L. Austin were in Cos. E, K, and D, respectively, of the 64th New York, Frank Robert's regiment. RG 94, Compiled Military Service Records, Pvt. Warren B. Parsons, Co. E; Pvt. Philip N. Austin, Co. K; and Pvt. Asa L. Austin, Co. D, 64th New York Infantry, National Archives.

2. Edwin R. Wakeman was one of Rosetta's aliases. It is possible that she took the new name because of her admiration for her Colonel, Edwin P. Davis.

*   *   *

Capitol Hill
Washington, D.C.
October the 31/63

Dear Father and Mother,

I receive you letter last night. I was glad to hear from you all once more. I am well and I feel thankful to God that he has spared my life and kept me in good health until the present time, and glad to hear that you have bought out that Cider mill in Church hollow and got it home. When I get my pay I will Send you what money I Can Spare if it ain't but a little. Tell mother I will send her that ring that I Showed to Henry Austin.

Our regiment expect to Stay here this winter. I would like to have you Send me a small box with iron hinges on it and a lock and key. Put the key inSide of the box and Screw the Cover on and when I get the box I Can draw the Screw and open the box and get the key. Then if I have anything, my goods friends won't Steal it. If you are a mind to Send me a piece of butter and Some Cakes, I will be very thankful to you.

Is Fon aliving with you yet or not? Please let me know. When I think of home it Seems like a dream to me, but Still I know there is Such a place as home that I left one year ago. It is but one Chance to ten that I ever Shall meet you again in this world. There is a good many temptations in the army. I got led away into this world So bad that I sinned a good deal. But I now believe that God Spirit has been aworking with me, and 'til that I was aComing back to Him again, and I hope and pray that I never shall be led away like it again.[1] I have a hope that if I never meet you again in this world that I Shall meet you in paradise where parting will be no more.

I got a letter from Frank a few days ago. He is not but a little ways from Alexandria. Some of our men have Stood guard where Frank is. Good-by for this time from,

Rosetta Wakeman

I thank you for them Stamps. Don't you ever ask me to lend you some money again in this world. If you do I won't send it to you.

---

1. A literal transcription of this passage reads: "I goot led a way into this world Sow bad that I Sind a good deal but I know be live that God Spirt has been a working with me and till that I was a Soming back to him a gain and I hope and pry that I never shall be led a way like it a gain."

Capitol Hill
Washington, D.C.
November the 22, 1863

Dear Father and Mother,

I take my time to write a few lines to you and let you [know] that I am well and I hope those few lines will find you all the same.

Our regiment is under marching orders and we expect to go to the front. Some think that we shall go to Tennessee. For my part I hope we shall go so far South that we Shan't freeze to death this winter. We have been relieve from all guard duty in the City. All the guards that we have now is are our Camp guard. We expect to Change our guns and get new ones before we leave Washington.

I got a letter from Frank yesterday. He is to Fairfax Seminary hospital near Alexandria, virginia. If we Stay here I shall get a pass and go see him, but we expect to go away this week. Willis is here in Washington but I don't know whether I Can get a pass and go and see him or not. If we stay here I shall go and try it.

I got my pay the other day but my Clothing bill was so much that I didn't get but 12 dollars and 50 cents, and I Can't let you have any of it, but when we get paid again and if I get money enough so I Can Spare it, I will Send you money. It Cost me a good deal to live for when I have got any money I will have something to eat, as long as I can get it.

I Can't think of any more to Write at present. So good-by for this time, from you Affectionate,

Rosetta Wakeman

*   *   *

Capitol Hill
Washington, D.C.
December the 9, 1863

Dear Father and Mother,

I take my pen in hand to let you know that I am well. I receive you letter about two weeks ago. I was glad to hear from you once more. The reason that I didn't write to you was this: We expect to go away from here every day, but now the prospect looks favorable I think that we Shall Stay here all winter. Our men has gone to guard Carroll Prison again this morning. We haven't had any Snow yet. It is pretty Cold [at] night but it is warm days. Congress Sat yesterday. It will last four months.

You may Send me a box as Soon as you are a mind to. Send me what things you are a mind to. I don't Care anything about any Cider nor wine. I would like Some butter if you have it to Spare, and Some pies. Direct you box to Washington, D.C. Send it by express.

Please let me know how much grain you have raised this year and how much pork you have butchered, and did you kill a beef this fall? If you did please send me a piece of dried beef.

So good-by from yours Affectionate,

Edwin R. Wakeman

Dear Mother,

I send you a Silver ring in this letter.[1] I hope you will get it. The ring cost me 75 cents.

I often think of the last hour that I Spent with you. You needn't think that I don't Care anything about you for I do. You are a mother yet. I would give all this world to Spend one more evening with you, but I don't know whether I ever Shall or not.

You needn't be afraid of our regiment ever going to the front for it never will as long as Col. Edwin P. Davis has the Command of the regiment. We are just as strict as any regulars that is in the army. Our guns have got to be polished So you can see your face in the barrel. When we come out on dress parade there isn't one man [who] dast to stir his foot or hand any, as the regiment is ordered to do, and then they have got to all make one motion at once. Our regiment is well thought of in this City. We Can make as good appearance as any regiment that is here in this City.

So good-by Dear Father, from your true love,

Rosetta Wakeman

---

1. This may be a reference to the ring that was found along with Rosetta's letters and daguerreotype. The ring is engraved with the words, "Rosetta Wakeman / 153rd N.Y. Vol. / Co. H." See photo, p. 57.

*   *   *

[*The following is the second of Frank R. Roberts' letters to the Wakeman family that was found among Rosetta's letters:*]

Camp of 64th Regiment, N.Y.V.
December 24, 1863

Dear Uncle, Aunt & Cousins,

I now take another opportunity to let you know how I am getting along. I am well with the exception of a hard cold. I am in hopes that these few lines will find you all well.

I received Aunt Emily's and Lois' letter and was glad to hear from you and hear that you was well. I hope that you will write often. I get two or three letters a week from home. I have not heard from Ritta in about two weeks.[1] I shall write her this afternoon. I hear from Willis often. He thinks that he will soon get his discharge. I hope he will.

Our regiment is now situated in the woods about five miles from Brandy Station. That is a station on the Orange & Alexandria RR. We are in winter quarters. We have houses made of logs covered with canvass, chimneys made of stone, and the first sight of the houses would convince a man that they were made by men that understood their business. But then, they will do. They are much better than none, especially in this cold weather.

The boys has just come off from picket. I shall have to

[*Here the letter is cut off at the bottom of the page, so the top of the other side is missing.*]

This is rather a dry letter. Write soon. My love to all.

Frank R. Roberts

Direct to:
Frank R. Roberts
Co. D, 64 N.Y.S.V.
Washington, D.C.

---

1. "Ritta" is Rosetta Wakeman.

*   *   *

Sgt. William Henry Austin,
109th Regiment, New York State Volunteers.

Photo courtesy of U.S. Army Military History Institute, Carlisle Barracks.

Rosetta Wakeman's ring, engraved with
"Rosetta Wakeman / Co. H / 153rd N.Y. Vol."

Photo courtesy of Mr. Jackson K. Doane.

Capitol Hill
Washington, D.C.
December the 28/63

Dear Father and Mother,

I receive you kind and welcome letter today. I am well and tough as a bear this winter. I receive a letter from Frank today. He is well at the time the letter was wrote.[1]

As for my Coming home on a furlough this winter I don't know whether I Can or not. There has a good many of our men has been home on a furlough. You needn't send me any box for I Can get along without one just as well as not.

We expect Some new recruits to fill up our regiment. When you write to me again let me know where fon is. Is he living with you this winter or not?

I don't care anything about Coming home for I [am] aShamed to Come, and I sometimes think that I never will go home in the world. I have enjoyed my self the best since I have been gone away from home than I ever did before in my life. I have had plenty of money to spend and a good time asoldier[ing]. I find just as good friends among Strangers as I do at home.

We haven't seen any snow here yet but it rains here today.

I sometimes think that I will re-enlist for five years and get my eight hundred dollars bounty. I Can do that if I am a mind to. What do you think about that?

I Can't think of any more to write. So good-by from your

Edwin R. Wakeman
or Rosetta Wakeman

---

1. Frank Roberts returned to active duty with the 64th New York from the U.S. Army General Hospital at Fairfax Seminary on December 10, 1863. He would not survive the war, however. He was taken prisoner at the Battle of Reams Station at the Weldon Railroad near the Petersburg lines in Virginia in August, 1864. He was never heard from again. RG 94, Compiled Military Service Records, Pvt. Frank R. Roberts, 64th New York Infantry, National Archives. Record Group 15, Pension File No. C222.100, Pvt. Franklin R. Roberts (filed by his mother, Susan), National Archives.

*   *   *

January, 1864–May, 1864

The new year brought passage of a bill re-establishing the Federal military rank of lieutenant general. It would be filled by a commander from the west who knew how to wage war on Southern armies and win. In the next year-and-a-half, Lt. Gen. Ulysses S. Grant would forge the Union's disparate armies into one destructive engine bent on forcing the South to its knees. Before Grant could take command, however, President Lincoln and General-in-Chief Henry Wager Halleck would "borrow" a portion of Federal forces one last time for some unfinished business.

Lincoln and Halleck had for some time been alarmed by France's interference in the affairs of Mexico. Convinced that a strong show of U.S. sovereignty over Texas must be demonstrated in order to forestall any future French attempts to annex U.S. territory, Halleck ordered Maj. Gen. Nathaniel P. Banks to establish a strong presence in that Confederate state. Banks, commanding the 19th and 13th Army Corps in New Orleans, had mounted two unsuccessful efforts to carry out these orders in 1863. His new plan involved striking northwest through the heart of Louisiana, following the Red River up to Shreveport near the Texas border.

With the entire Mississippi River now in Federal hands, Confederate territory to the west of the river was cut off from its central seat of power in Richmond, making operations in the Trans-Mississippi territory of little strategic value in the war on the Confederacy. Grant preferred to employ Banks' army to move east on Mobile to tighten the noose on the main Confederate armies, but Banks' orders had been issued by Halleck prior to the change in high command. Giving his reluctant assent to the plan, Grant imposed an April deadline for its completion and the return of the additional troops Banks borrowed from Maj. Gen. William T. Sherman to pursue his plan.

The deciding factor leading Banks, a former governor of Massachusetts, to undertake his third campaign for Texas was the possibility of finally making himself a war hero--by presenting to Washington the cotton stores that could be seized along his invasion route. Cotton and the liberation of enough Union sympathizers to bring Louisiana representation back into the U.S. Congress would ensure his post-war candidacy for high office, or so went Banks' reasoning.

Thus the stage was set for an arduous, costly, and ultimately unsuccessful expedition up Louisiana's Red River.

*   *   *

Capitol Hill
Washington, D.C.
January the 20/64

Dear Father,

I take this present Opportunity to answer you kind and welcome letter that I receive yesterday. I was glad to hear from home once more and learn that you and the rest of the family was all well. I am well at present and enjoy the best of health.

I accept of your advice very kindly.[1] My mind is not easy at any time. For my part I can see the principle of the men in this regiment, and I have chosen the better part. We have got some just as good men in my company as there is to be found in the state of new york. They use me well and I try to use them as I would like to be used. Some of our men has been punished very bad, but for my part I haven't been punished Since I have been in the service. I never got to fighting but once. Then Mr. Stephen Wiley pitched on me and I give him three or four pretty good cracks and he put downstairs with him Self.[2]

As for coming home, I Shall come if I live long enough. You mustn't look for me until you see me where you are.

I wish you would write a letter for Robert to me and let me know how he feels about me. Tell Robert I would like to see him or have him with me. I hope the day will come when we all can meet in this world once more but I can't come home this winter, for they have let some go home and they haven't come back yet. Now they won't let any more go home out of my company.[3]

It is getting almost dinner time. The bugle has just blowed for dinner. I send my best respect to you and all inquiring friends.

So good-by from your Affectionate friend,

Edwin R. Wakeman

1. Rosetta's original reads, "I exped of your advice very kindly."

2. Pvt. Stephen Wiley was one of the troublemakers of the 153rd. He was court-martialed three times in as many months in the fall of 1863, twice for drunkenness while on duty and once for theft. Apparently, he was no match for the diminutive Rosetta, even though he was seven inches taller than she. RG 94, Regimental Order Book, 153rd New York Infantry, National Archives; RG 94, Regimental Descriptive Book, Company H, 153rd New York Infantry, National Archives.

3. Rosetta's pleas that she could not get a furlough to come home were rather disingenuous. She could have gone home at any time upon revealing her true identity to army officials.

*   *   *

Headquarters, Dept. of Washington[1]
22nd Army Corps, Washington, D.C.
February 16, 1864

General,

The Major General Commanding directs that the 153rd Regiment, New York Volunteers be prepared for immediate service in the field. The Regiment will move by transport.

By command of
Major Gen. [C. C.] Augur

1. RG 94, Regimental Order Book, 153rd New York Infantry, National Archives.

*   *   *

Headquarters 153rd NY Vols.[1]
Washington, D.C.
February 16th, 1864

General Order }
No. 9 }

Company Commanders will prepare their men
to move at a moment's notice. No Guards will be relieved until
further orders from HeadQuarters. The men will be provided
with haversacks, canteens & knapsacks complete. Company
commanders will make immediate requisitions for all deficien-
cies in clothing &c. The men will carry with them their dress
clothing & blouses. Company Commanders will immediately
report how many men they can take with them & draw the
necessary arms & equipments for all recruits.

By order of
Edwin P. Davis, Colonel

---

1. RG 94, Regimental Order Book, 153rd New York Infantry,
National Archives.

* * *

Headquarters, Miltary Dist. of Wash.[1]
Washington, D.C.
February 17th, 1864

General,
The Major General Commanding directs that
the 153rd N.Y.V. march to Alexandria so as to arrive there for
embarkation at 5 o'clock tomorrow afternoon. In case there
should be any delay in the transportation, the Regiment can
stay at the Soldier's Rest, Alexandria, overnight . . . .

I am, General,
Very Respectfully,
Your Obedient Servant,
Sw. Adv. Reymond, A.A. Genl

---

1. RG 94, Regimental Order Book, 153rd New York Infantry,
National Archives.

* * *

Capitol Hill
Washington, D.C.
February the 18/64

Dear Father,

    I write a few lines to you to let you know that I am well.
Our regiment is agoing to leave Washington today. We are
agoing to texas by the way of new orleans. We are agoing to
take the boat at Alexandria.
    I bid you all good-by. Don't never expect to see you again.
Edwin R. Wakeman

*   *   *

HeadQuarters 153rd New York Vols.[1]
Soldiers' Rest, Alexandria, Va
February 19th, 1864

Special Order }
No. 12   }

    *The Regiment will embark on board the Steam
Ship* Mississippi. *Companies A, F, D and G will occupy the
lower bunks, lower deck. Adjutant Major [Alexander] Strain
will be in charge of this deck. Five (5) men to each bunk. The
officers of each company will see that their men are properly
provided for, and that no more room is used than what is
actually necessary for the men. Companies I, C, H, E, K, G &
B will occupy the upper bunks, upper deck. An officer of the
day will be appointed for each deck. The 153rd will occupy the
forward part of the ship.*

By order of
Edwin P. Davis, Colonel

---

    1. RG 94, Regimental Order Book, 153rd New York Infantry,
National Archives.

*   *   *

HeadQuarters 153rd New York Vols.[1]
Steam Ship Mississippi
February 25th, 1864

General Order   }
No. 15   }

> *Commanders of companies will cause their men to strip and wash themselves thoroughly. They will use the buckets that have been furnished them or a hose if practicable, and commence immediately.*

By order of Edwin P. Davis

---

1. Unfortunately, we have no way of knowing how Rosetta dealt with the challenge presented to her by this order. In that modest age, however, it is likely that "strip" meant only down to one's long johns. RG 94, Regimental Order Book, 153rd New York Infantry, National Archives.

*   *   *

State of Louisiana,
City of Algiers[1]
March the 2/64

Dear Father and Mother,

I take the first time I could get to write to you and let you know that I am well.

We left washington the 18 of feb. and marched to Alexandria. We left Alexandria the 20 and got to new Orleans the last day of february. We landed in the City of Algiers the 29 of february. I was nine days on the water and six days out of sight of land. Where we shall go from here I don't know.

We have made our quarters in an Old Machine Shop. When we left Washington we left home and have gone outdoors to live.

I got Robert's likeness and it looks like him. The artist that took Robert likeness didn't half finish it off and it rub some and that made it look bad. I would like to stand over him with a load[ed] gun and fix[ed] bayonet and learn him how to take a likeness.

I saw Henry Austin in Alexandria, va. and bid him good-by for the last time.

I shouldn't be surprised if we went to Mobile.[2] There they expect a fight before long, for our regiment has gone to raising hell so much that we will get shove to the field of battle. If they had behave themselves we might have stayed at Washington all summer. Some of Co. E men got to fighting with the Police men, and it wasn't but a few day before we started for new orleans.[3] I don't never expect to see one of you again in this world. If we never meet here on earth again, I hope I shall meet you all in heaven where parting will be no more.

Direct you letter to new orleans, State of Louisiana. So good by from yours of late,

Edwin R. Wakeman

---

1. The City of Algiers lies across the Mississippi River from New Orleans, Louisiana.

2. The 19th Corps was ordered to prepare for a protracted campaign in early March, but the rank and file were not informed of the object of the campaign for several days, and in one regiment's case, for over a week. Camp rumor maintained that the 19th Corps would march on Mobile, Alabama, though in fact they were preparing for a campaign up the Red River. Dr. Harris H. Beecher, *Record of the 114th Regiment New York State Volunteers*, (Norwich, NY: J.R. Hubbard, Jr., 1866), pp. 290-292.

3. While Rosetta's supposition about the 153rd's transfer to the field seems plausible, there is nothing in the 153rd's regimental orders, letters, or other books and documents to support her theory.

*   *   *

Franklin City
Louisiana
March the 8/64

Dear Father and Mother,

I take my time to write a few lines to you tonight and let you know where I am. I am in Camp at Franklin, LA. I am well and enjoy good health and I hope those few lines will find you all the same.

Our regiment has join the first Brigade and first Division and 19 army Corps under the command of major General Banks. We expect to march Soon for Alexandria [Louisiana] and the red river. We expect to have some fighting to do before we get there to the red river. I don't never expect to see you again in this world. I bid henry Austin good-by when I was in Alexandria, Va. I got Robert likeness when I was in Washington.

The weather is as warm here as it is in N.Y. the first of June. The trees is in full bloom and the grass is quite high.

I can't think of any more to write at present. So good-by from your Affectionate

Edwin R.L. Wakeman[1]

Direct you letter to New Orleans, LA.
    Co. H., 153rd Regiment, N.Y.S. Vol.
    First Brigade
    First Division and
    19 Army Corps
    R.L. Wakeman in the care of
    Capt. McLaughlin

---

1. "Edwin" is written in directly over "Rosetta," in an attempt to cover it over.

*   *   *

The 19th Corps, two divisions of the 13th Corps, and a division of cavalry, together numbering close to 20,000 soldiers, departed from Franklin, Louisiana on the 15th of March. Their first objective was 180 miles away at Alexandria, where they would join elements of the 16th and 17th Corps under command of Brig. Gen. A.J. Smith. The combined land force would be complemented by R. Adm. David P. Porter's naval fleet, which was steaming up the Red River to Alexandria from the Mississippi. From there General Banks' plan called for the entire expedition to travel another 170 miles northwest up the Red River to take Shreveport.

Charged by Banks to organize the movement from Franklin to Alexandria, Maj. Gen. William B. Franklin issued General Order No. 19, which read, in part: "No woman shall accompany the command except by express authority from these HeadQuarters given upon written application through the ordinary channels."[1]

Franklin, no doubt, was referring to laundresses, cooks, nurses, "daughters" of regiments, officers' wives, and other camp followers, never suspecting that a woman might be in uniform.

The true irony of Franklin's order is that Rosetta Wakeman was not the only woman to "accompany the command" on this campaign without "express authority." Brig. Gen. A.J. Smith's troops at Alexandria contained another woman soldier who would be incorporated into Banks' army--Pvt. Albert D.J. Cashier, 95th Illinois Infantry, Second Brigade, 17th Army Corps. Private Cashier happened to be a young Irish immigrant whose true identity was Jennie Hodgers.[2]

Rosetta's command reached Alexandria, Louisiana on March 25, 1864, after a ten-day march covering an average of eighteen miles a day.

1. RG 94, Order Book of the 153rd New York Infantry, National Archives.
2. RG 94, Compiled Military Service Record, Pvt. Albert D.J. Cashier, 95th Illinois Infantry, National Archives; and RG 15, Pension File #C-2,573248, based on the service of Pvt. Albert D.J. Cashier, National Archives.

* * *

Alexandria
LA
March the 27/64

Dear Father and Mother,

I take my time to write a few lines to you and let you know that I am well and I hope those few lines will find you the Same.

I have marched two hundred miles. We was ten days on the road amarching. We expect to Start for Shreveport tomorrow. Today is Sunday. We arrived here [at Alexandria] Saturday.

I send my best respect to you all. So good-by from,

E. R. Wakeman

Direct you letter to New Orleans, L.A. Write soon and let me know how you all get along.

from Edwin R. Wakeman

* * *

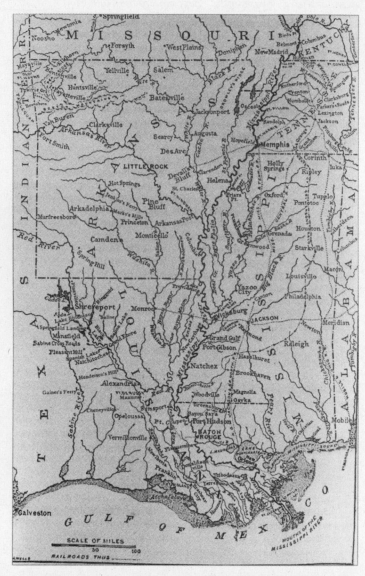

Map of the Red River, Arkansas, and Missouri Campaigns of 1864.
From Battles & Leaders of the Civil War, Vol. IV, p. 348.

After resting for two days at Alexandria, Rosetta's regiment continued on to Natchitoches, covering over 70 miles in the next six days. They off-loaded supplies and forage from Porter's river transports for three days at nearby Grand Ecore Landing. Banks' troops continued to press forward on April 6. Taking a road that swung out and away to the west of the Red River, Banks' army, which measured a day's march from end to end with 12 miles of wagons to guard, covered another 43 miles in the next two-and-a-half days. The entire column filed along a narrow road through a dense pine forest, a careless and perilous disposition of troops so deep in enemy territory. Confederate skirmishers disputed each advance of the Federal cavalry at the head of the column.

At Sabine Cross Roads, a Confederate force of 11,000 under the command of Maj. Gen. Richard Taylor lay in wait for the Federals. Taylor had served under Stonewall Jackson in the 1862 Shenandoah Valley Campaign, and shared that general's audacity. The opportunity that the long, narrow, forest-bordered Federal column presented to Taylor was too much to resist, even though he was under orders from Gen. Edmond Kirby Smith, commander of the Trans-Mississippi Department, not to bring about a general engagement. On April 8, Taylor attacked the unsupported Union cavalry in the van of the march, throwing them back in confusion. The 13th Corps was rushed forward to meet the Confederate threat, only to be broken. Banks then ordered the 19th Corps up to stop the Union rout. The veterans of the 19th formed a line of battle across the road in a forest clearing, allowing the defeated and demoralized men of the cavalry and 13th Corps to rush past them to the rear. When the oncoming Confederate charge met the volleys of the well-disciplined 19th Corps, their victorious advance was halted. Rosetta's regiment was detailed to guard the division wagon train while the Battle of Sabine Cross Roads raged several miles away.

Early in the morning of April 9, the 153rd New York rejoined the First Brigade, First Division, 19th Corps and retraced their steps eight miles to Pleasant Hill. There they took up a defensive position at 8:00 a.m. The 153rd waited for hours for the enemy onslaught while the Confederate artillery pounded away. When it came, the 19th Corps bore the brunt of the Confederate attack, and Private Wakeman stood to her task through numerous Confederate assaults. By most reports Taylor had the advantage in numbers, but the Federals had the advantage of position, and the Union troops carried the day.

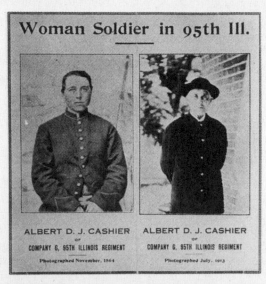

Woman Soldier in 95th Ill.

ALBERT D. J. CASHIER
OF
COMPANY G, 95TH ILLINOIS REGIMENT

Photographed November, 1864

ALBERT D. J. CASHIER
OF
COMPANY G, 95TH ILLINOIS REGIMENT

Photographed July, 1913

Jennie Hodgers, alias Pvt. Albert D.J. Cashier, another woman soldier who took part in the Red River Campaign.

Photo courtesy of the Illinois State Historical Society.

Deck of the Steamship *Mississippi,* taken May 30, 1864.

Photo courtesy of National Archives.

Private Wakeman was in the front lines and in the fiercest fighting during the four-hour Battle of Pleasant Hill, which ended with darkness. She lay on her arms on the battlefield that evening and listened to the pitiful cries of the wounded and dying. At midnight, the Union army began its 40-mile retreat back to Grand Ecore Landing, arriving there on April 11. On April 14, Rosetta wrote her last letter home.

*   *   *

Grand Ecore Landing, LA [1]
on the Red River
April the 14/64

Dear Mother and Father, Brothers and Sisters,

I take my time to write a few lines to you. I am well and in good spirit and I hope those few lines will find you all the same.

Our army made an advance up the river to pleasant hill about 40 miles. There we had a fight. The first day of the fight our army got whip[ped] and we had to retreat back about ten miles. The next day the fight was renewed and the firing took place about eight o'Clock in the morning. There was a heavy Cannonading all day and a Sharp firing of infantry. I was not in the first day's fight but the next day I had to face the enemy bullets with my regiment. I was under fire about four hours and laid on the field of battle all night. There was three wounded in my Co. and one killed. [2]

Albert Weathermax wounded in the head. Ranson Conklin wounded through the hip. Edwin West had one of his fingers shot off. [3] Joseph Blanchard killed. That is all that was hurt in my Co.

I feel thankful to God that he spared my life and I pray to him that he will lead me safe through the field of battle and that I may return safe home.

I receive you kind and welcome letter the other day. I was glad to learn that you was agoing to work the Ham farm this summer and milk twenty cows. I would advise you to buy the farm and if you will, I will Come home and help you pay for it, if I live to get out of the army. By that time Robert will be big enough to do a good days work and he and my Self can work both of them farm like everything.

I can't think of any more to write at present. So good-by from you Affectionate,

Edwin R. Wakeman

Direct to New Orleans, LA. when you write again. Write all the particulars about that farm and let me know how much stock you have got to keep this summer and how many Calves you raise and how many hogs you have got.

Edwin R. Wakeman

Grand Ecore Landing, LA

I got a letter from Frank and he stated that you had bought the Ham farm and when you write to me again I want to know the whole particulars about it, and how is that railroad get[ting] along this Spring?

I wrote in this letter that Joseph Blanchard was killed but he is not. He was taken prisoner and got away from them and came to his Co. and regiment this afternoon.

Edwin R. Wakeman

---

1. Banks' command spent the days of April 11 through 21 at Grand Ecore Landing, above Natchitoches on the Red River. Rosetta spelled words as she heard them, and in the case of "Grand Ecore," she heard "Brandycore," which is the heading that appears on her original letter.

2. Here Rosetta describes the part taken by the 153rd in the Union loss at Sabine Cross Roads on April 8 and in the Battle of Pleasant Hill, which occurred the next day on April 9. Reports of Maj. Gen. William B. Franklin of operations on April 6-25, *The War of Rebellion: A Compilation of Official Records of the Union and Confederate Armies*, Series I, Vol. 34, Part 1, Reports, (Washington: Government Printing Office1880-1901), pp. 256-262. Also, Report of Edwin P. Davis, Colonel commanding the 153rd New York, pp. 425-426.

3. Medical records for these men confirm Rosetta's report of their injuries. Surprisingly, Weathermax recovered from a severe head wound and returned to duty with the 153rd in July. Conklin and West spent over a month in U.S.A. General Hospital in New Orleans before being furloughed in mid-May, just before Rosetta arrived there on May 22. RG 94, Carded Medical Records, Volunteers, Mexican & Civil Wars, 1846-1865, 153rd New York Infantry, National Archives.

*   *   *

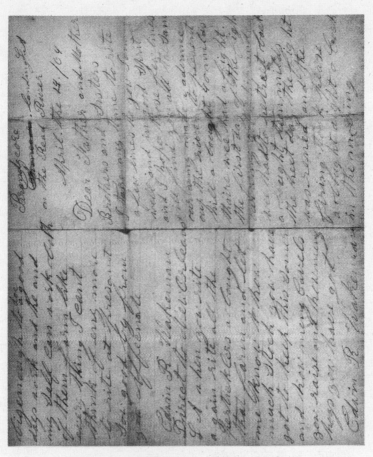

Detail of Rosetta Wakeman's April 14, 1864 letter.
Photo courtesy of Mr. Jackson K. Doane.

Headquarters 153 Regt. N.Y. Vols.[1]
Grand Ecore April 12, 1864

Capt. Oliver Mathews
Assistant Adjutant General

Captain,

I have the honor to submit the following report of the Campaign since we left Natchitoches: On the morning of the 6th instant (Wednesday) I broke camp at Natchitoches at 7:30 a.m., joined my Brigade, and took up a line of march in direction of Pleasant Hill. After proceeding about 17 miles we bivouacked for the night at 5:30 p.m. At 5:30 a.m. of Thursday, the 7th instant, we broke camp and took up the line of march; reached Pleasant Hill about 4 p.m. and went into bivouac about 5 p.m. Heard firing in our front and rumors of our Cavalry having engaged the enemy.

The next morning, being Friday, we broke camp at 6 o'clock a.m. My Regiment was detached from the Brigade, being detailed as Rear Guard to the Division trains to relieve the 30th Maine Volunteers, which I did at 11 o'clock that day. At 3 o'clock p.m. I reached the old saw mill where the First Brigade had gone into bivouac, but soon the Division moved forward and my Regiment was ordered to remain and guard the wagons and artillery which were left in Camp at the old saw mill, which I did.

The next morning at 4 o'clock a.m., the 9th instant, I rejoined my Brigade at the old saw mill and took the rear of the column en route for Pleasant Hill, where we arrived at 8 1/2 o'clock a.m. of same day, and took up a position in the woods on the right of the main road, where I remained until 5 o'clock p.m., when I received orders to move my Regiment up the main road leading from Pleasant Hill and to take up a position, the right of my regiment resting on the road, and the line of Battle directly diagonal across the woods; also to throw out my skirmishers with orders to hold their position and not to fire a shot until the enemy made their appearance in strong force.

I had been here but a short time when the enemy made their appearance in a strong force, drove in my skirmishers, and fired in a terrific volley into my Regiment, which was handsomely met by my men, who poured volley after volley and succeeded in driving them out of the woods. Again they made their appearance and endeavored to turn my regiment and left flank, but were driven back pell mell. They again made several attempts to drive me from *my position without success. I maintained it until I was ordered to retire, my ammunition being all exhausted, about 8 o'clock, and took up a new position in the rear and about 40 yards to the left. About 2 a.m. of the 10th instant I joined the Brigade and took our line of march for Grand Ecore. We Bivouacked about 2 o'clock on Sunday, the 10th instant, for the night. Broke camp at 5.50 of the morning of the 11th instant and reached Grand Ecore at 3 1/2 p.m.*

My men behaved nobly, and I attach much credit to the noble manner in which my line officers acted, and Lt. Col. Strain, Major Sammons, & Adjutant Davis rendered me valuable assistance in keeping my line together and maintaining my position.

The Casualties are as follows:

1 killed
28 wounded
12 missing

Respectfully,
Edwin P. Davis
Colonel

---

1. RG 94, Regimental Letter Book, 153rd New York Infantry, National Archives. This letter also appears in *The War of the Rebellion: Official Records of the Union and Confederate Armies*, Series I, Volume 34, Part I Reports, pp. 425-426.

*   *   *

Epilogue

The Battle of Pleasant Hill was a tactical victory for General Banks that recouped many of the guns and supplies that had been lost to Confederate General Taylor's troops the previous day at Sabine Cross Roads. It was clear, however, that the entire Red River campaign was flawed and failing. Despite the time of year, the water level of the Red River continued to fall, threatening to prevent the safe return of Admiral Porter's fleet to the Mississippi River. The deadline had passed for return of Brig. Gen. A.J. Smith's 16th and 17th Corps to Sherman's army for the spring general offensive planned by Grant. Banks' lieutenants advised a halt to any renewed forward movement up the Red River, and a return to Grand Ecore Landing to rest and reevaluate the situation.

Rosetta wrote her final letter home on April 14, 1864, while the 153rd New York was entrenched at Grand Ecore with the rest of Banks' army. On April 21 they learned that elements of Taylor's forces had gotten around their rear farther down the river. As a result, at ten o'clock on that evening, the army began a 70-mile retreat to Alexandria by forced march. All that night and the following day they trudged, while the enemy harassed their rear guard. Once the 19th Corps was halted to form a line of battle, but the expected attack didn't materialize. On they marched. By midnight of April 22 they had covered 35 miles in 14 hours, having stopped only once for a meal.

"It was a terrible march, trying to the utmost the endurance of every man," said one participant. "Scores were unable to keep up, and with an utter disregard for life, they fell out of the column unable to move further. One man . . . dropped dead on that march from exhaustion."[1] Whether set by undisciplined Federal soldiers or by Rebel sympathizers signaling the line of Union retreat, houses and barns burned day and night throughout their journey.[2] At one o'clock in the morning the army halted for a brief rest, but were awakened again at four a.m. to resume the forced march. As one veteran of Banks' Louisiana campaigns wrote, "the truth is, that Banks is the most merciless marcher of men that I ever knew."[3]

At sunrise on the 23rd they reached Monett's Bluff and the Cane River crossing, where they found the enemy in a strong position on the opposite high bank, with "their Baterys planted & the Best natural position in the state of La."[4] Rosetta's brigade was ordered to lie down in the woods on the Union side of the river and wait for the Third Brigade to ford the river three miles north and attack the Confederate left flank. Taylor's artillery began a vigorous shelling of Union positions as Rosetta and her comrades stationed themselves. They were forced to lie in wait for several hours while subjected to a constant bombardment by the Confederate guns. Meanwhile, the sound of artillery far to the Union rear signaled that A.J. Smith's troops were engaged in fending off a large Rebel force. The Union army was now surrounded and trapped. These, said one soldier alarmed by the army's precarious situation, were some of the most anxious hours of the entire Red River campaign. "A general despondency pervaded the whole army," wrote another, for "We were hundreds of miles from our supplies, successfully checked by the enemy, at a point of his own choosing; [and] with another force he was thundering in our rear and pressing our column."[5]

Late in that afternoon the Third Brigade made its assault on the Confederate position across the river. Fierce fighting ensued for over an hour. Rosetta's First Brigade was ordered to charge the Confederate force in a frontal attack. "We skirmished double quick out in to the open field & followed the Cavalry across the river & took possession of the ground that the Rebs had held all day," wrote Capt. John H. Lassell of the 153rd.[6] At the same time the sound of battle in the rear died down, and all rejoiced at having extricated themselves from a very bad situation.

Within an hour of this engagement, Union engineers built a pontoon bridge across the Cane River. The army passed over and continued its march until midnight.

The retreat resumed at six a.m. on Sunday, April 24th. Much of the day was wasted, though, upon discovery that the army had taken a wrong road in the pine woods and was lost. "Such a dilemma could not find a parallel in the history of the war. An army of over

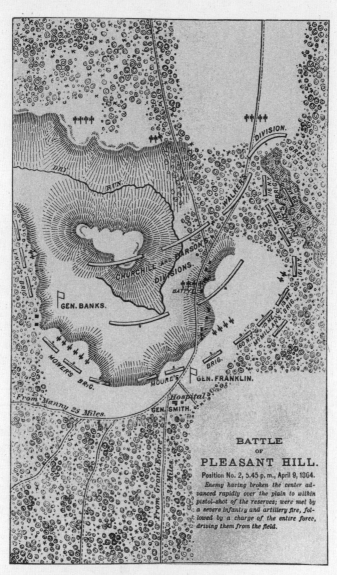

Battle of Pleasant Hill.

From Official Records, *Series I, Vol. 34, Part 1, Reports, p. 231.*

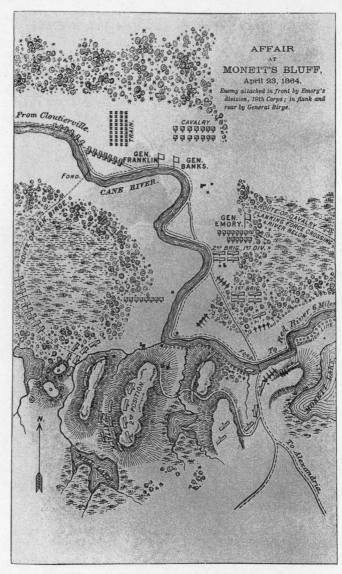

Engagement at Monett's Bluff.
From Official Records, Series I, Vol. 34, Part 1, Reports, p. 233.

forty thousand men had actually become *lost in the woods* [emphasis in the original],''[7] wrote one wag. At length they marched on, covering approximately 18 miles and bivouacking at Henderson's Bluff for the night.

Another march of 19 miles on an extremely hot and dusty April 25th brought Banks' weary troops to rest in Alexandria. Here the army was reunited with Admiral Porter's naval force, which had come down the river from Grand Ecore. By now the Red River had fallen so low that Porter's ironclads, gunboats, and transports were unable to cross over the rapids above Alexandria. While the army and navy high command were engaged in studying this alarming turn of events, Rosetta and her comrades settled into camp just north of town.

While plans developed to get the ironclads and gunboats over the river rapids above Alexandria, Rosetta fell ill. She had persevered through almost 400 miles of hard marching, camping, and fighting in a subtropical climate. To the exertions of the march were added the bad water and the unpalatable and infrequent meals that soldiers on campaign endured. Assistant Surgeon Beecher of the 114th New York wrote that ''The effect of this [Louisiana] climate upon the new Regiments was truly appalling. While the acclimated members of the 114th were enjoying a complete immunity from disease, all around was daily heard the death march of military funerals. Scurvy and chronic diarrhea were carrying off thousands of victims to untimely graves.''[8]

Rosetta would soon number among these victims. She was admitted to the 153rd Regimental Hospital on May 3, complaining of chronic diarrhea, the most deadly disease of the Civil War.[9] On May 7, she was sent to the Marine U.S.A. General Hospital in New Orleans. Unlike her wounded comrades Ransom Conklin and Edward West, whose trips to New Orleans from the Pleasant Hill battlefield took only five days, Rosetta's voyage from Alexandria to New Orleans took 15 days, and she was not admitted to the general hospital until May 22.[10]

There is one likely explanation for Rosetta's lengthy trip. On May 5, two days before Rosetta set out for the New Orleans hospital, Rebel troops attacked and destroyed three river transports several miles down the river from Alexandria, effectively closing off river traffic to the Mississippi for the next week and a half.[11] Inability to use the water route undoubtedly forced army surgeons to arrange for transport of the sick to general hospitals in ambulances and wagons. A 350-mile overland journey to New Orleans would account for the inordinately long time between Rosetta's discharge from the 153rd's Regimental hospital and her admission to the general hospital. A trip of this length, in uncomfortable conveyances over rough roads, would have further weakened anyone with Rosetta's disease. By the time she reached New Orleans, her condition was no longer chronic, but acute.[12]

One of the Federal transports destroyed by the Confederates was carrying soldiers' letters home. These missives were gleefully ransacked by the Confederates. Later in May, when Banks' army moved past this area on its final journey to the Mississippi, they would find their mail torn and strewn on the banks of the river.[13] Perhaps among the destroyed correspondence was a last letter home from Rosetta Wakeman.

Rosetta reached Marine U.S.A. General Hospital, located in the New Orleans Barracks, on May 22.[14] She occupied one of the 5,808 Federal army hospital beds established in the City of New Orleans by 1864.[15] Rosetta lingered for almost a month before succumbing on June 19, 1864. Despite the wasting disease that would have left her incapable of moving from her bed or attending to her own sanitary needs, her secret was never discovered, or at least was never reported by stewards or nurses to hospital surgeons, who surely would have made some note on her medical records.[16] Given the lack of medical knowledge at the time about the causes and cures for disease, it is unlikely that she received close examination by a doctor or a treatment regimen any more aggressive, invasive, or effective than bed rest. She numbers among 200,000 deaths from disease of Union soldiers, sailors, and marines during the war, which number is well over half of total Union military deaths.[17]

News of Private Wakeman's fate did not reach the 153rd New York until August of 1864. A note on her record indicates that a final statement with an inventory of her effects was sent to the Adjutant General's Office in December. Although it is unknown how word of Private Wakeman's end made its way to her family, her death was reported by Wakeman family members to New York State Census enumerators. The 1865 Census in Chenango County included data on soldiers who had died as a result of army service in the War of the Rebellion, as reported to their families. Private Lyons Wakeman, 21 years of age, is listed among these casualties.[18]

Sarah Rosetta Wakeman was given a soldier's burial in Chalmette National Cemetery in New Orleans. On her headstone is her enlisted name, Lyons Wakeman.[19]

I certify, on honor, that *Lyons Wakeman* a *Privat* of Captain *L.H. Laughlins* Company (*H*) of the *153* Regiment of *Infantry* VOLUNTEERS, of the State of *New York* born in *Afton* State of *New York*, aged *21* years; *5* feet *inches high; *fair* complexion, *blue* eyes, *brown* hair, and by occupation a *boatman*, having joined the company on its original organization at *Fonda N.Y.* and enrolled in it at the muster into the service of the United States at *Fonda N.Y.*, on the *17th* day of *October*, 186 2, (or was mustered in service as a recruit, by ____ , at ____ , on the ____ day of ____ , 186 , or was drafted and mustered into the service of the United States from the ____ Enrollment District of the State of ____ , at ____ , on the ____ day of ____ , 186 ,) to serve in the Regiment, for the term of *three years*, ____ ; and having served HONESTLY and FAITHFULLY with his Company in *the field* to the present date, is now entitled to a **DISCHARGE** by reason of *heart died in marine US.A General Hospital at New Orleans La on the 19 day of June 1864 of Chronic Diarrhoea*

The said *Privat Lyons Wakeman* was last paid by Paymaster *Maj. Mason* to include the *31st* day of *December*, 186 3, and has pay due him from that time to the present date; he is entitled to pay and subsistence for TRAVELING to place of enrollment, and whatever other allowances are authorized to volunteer soldiers, drafted men, or militia, so discharged. He has received from the United States **CLOTHING** amounting to *32 99* dollars, since the *1st* day of *November*, 186 3, when his clothing account was last settled. He has received from the United States *25* dollars advanced **BOUNTY**.

There is to be stopped from him, on account of the State of ____ , or other authorities, for **CLOTHING**, &c., received on entering service, ____ dollars; and for other stoppages, viz: ____

____ dollars.

He has been furnished with TRANSPORTATION in kind from the place of his discharge to ____ ; and he has been SUBSISTED for TRAVELING to his place of enrollment, up to the ____ , 186 .

He is indebted to *Henry M Hale*, BUTLER, *11 99* dollars.
He is indebted to ____ , LAUNDRESS, ____ dollars.

Given in Duplicate, at *Camp Bushell Va*, this *21st* day of *December*, 1864.

C.H. Pike

N. Lieut

Commanding Company.

[A. G. O. No. 95—PRVT.]

Pvt. Lyons Wakeman's army discharge.
Photo courtesy of National Archives.

Gates of Chalmette National Cemetery near New Orleans, Louisiana.

Photo by Donald Stout.

Pvt. Lyons Wakeman's headstone in Chalmette National Cemetery.

Photo by Donald Stout.

Had she survived the Red River ordeal, she would have defended Washington, D.C. during Lt. Gen. Jubal Early's invasion of Maryland in 1864, fought with General Sheridan in the Shenandoah Valley and perhaps witnessed Sheridan's famous ride from Winchester to Cedar Creek, and marched down Pennsylvania Avenue with victorious Union troops in the Grand Review of the Armies held in May, 1865. And, like Pvt. Albert Cashier and others, having gotten the taste of freedom and independence that wearing pants afforded her, perhaps Rosetta would have maintained her male disguise after the war and bought her farm in "Wisconsin. On the Prairie."

We may never know if other, unrecognized women lie among the 12,000 Civil War soldiers buried at Chalmette with Private Wakeman. We can be certain, though, that among the hundreds of thousands of military graves filled during that terrible conflict, many more women like Rosetta Wakeman, who answered their countries' calls in a time of crisis, lie undiscovered under headstones bearing their male enlisted names.

Notes

1. Orton S. Clark, *The 116th Regiment of New York State Volunteers,* (Buffalo, NY: Matthews & Warren, 1868), p. 167.

2. Both sides claimed the other caused the fires and destruction of property that occurred during Banks' retreat. Elias P. Pellet, *History of the 114th Regiment, New York State Volunteers,* (Norwich, NY: Telegraph & Chronicle Power Press, 1866), pp. 224-225. Clark, p. 166. Harris H. Beecher, *Record of the 114th Regiment, New York State Volunteers,* (Norwich, NY: J. F. Hubbard, Jr., Publisher, 1866), p. 330. Richard Taylor, *Destruction and Reconstruction: Personal Reminiscences of the Late War,* (New York: D. Appleton & Company, 1879), p. 193.

3. John W. DeForest, "Forced Marches in the Teche Country," in Henry Steele Commager, *The Blue & The Gray,* Vol. I, (Indianapolis: Bobbs-Merrill, 1950), p. 426.

4. Capt. John H. Lassell (James F. Morrison, ed.), *Boys in Blue of Company F, 153rd Regiment New York State Volunteers, Civil War Diary of John H. Lassell,* p. 11. Montgomery County Department of History and Archives, Fonda, NY.

5. Pellet, p. 226.

6. Lassell, p. 11.

7. Beecher, p. 336.

8. Diarrhea and dysentery, acute and chronic, caused 44,558 Union soldier deaths, more than any other disease. Data from the Medical and Surgical History of the War of the Rebellion, Vol. I, Part I, as quoted in Paul E. Steiner, *Disease in the Civil War,* (Springfield, IL: Charles C. Thomas, 1968), pp. 10-11.

9. Beecher, pp. 361-362.

10. RG 94, Carded Medical Records, Mexican and Civil Wars 1846-1865, Pvt. Lyons Wakeman, Co. H, 153rd New York Infantry, Volunteers, National Archives.

11. Taylor, p. 186. Beecher, pp. 347.

12. RG 94, Carded Medical Records, Mexican and Civil Wars 1846-1865, Pvt. Lyons Wakeman, Co. H, 153rd New York Infantry, Volunteers, National Archives.

13. Frank M. Flinn, *Campaigning with Banks and Sheridan,* (Lynn, MA: Press of Thomas P. Nichols, 1887), p. 145. Beecher, pp. 347-348.

14. Powell A. Casey, *Encyclopedia of Forts, Posts, Named Camps, and Other Military Installations in Louisiana, 1700-1981,* (Baton Rouge, LA: Claitor's Publishing Division, 1981), pp. 116-117.

15. Carl Moneyhon and Bobby Roberts, *Portraits of Conflict: A Photographic History of Louisiana in the Civil War*, (Fayetteville and London: Univ. of Arkansas Press, 1990), p. 257.

16. Records of the U.S.A. Marine General Hospital no longer exist. However, Pvt. Lyons Wakeman's medical and service records do not indicate that Rosetta was ever discovered to be a female. RG 94, Compiled Military Service Record, Pvt. Lyons Wakeman, National Archives. RG 15, Carded Medical Records, Volunteers, Mexican & Civil Wars, 1846-1865, Pvt. Lyons Wakeman, Co. H, 153rd New York Infantry, National Archives.

17. Frederick H. Dyer, *A Compendium of the War of Rebellion*, Vol. I, (New York: Thomas Yoseloff, [1908] 1959), p. 12.

18. Mrs. Edwin P. Smith, *Vital Records of Chenango County, New York Before 1880*, (Norwich, NY: Chenango County Historical Society, 1972), p. 5; 1865 New York State Census, *List of death of officers and enlisted men that occurred while in military or naval service of the U.S. or from wound or disease acquired in said service since April 1861, reported to families to which deceased belonged when at home in the Town of Afton.* Office of the Chenango County Clerk, Norwich, NY.

19. The death certificate included in Rosetta's army service record indicates that she was buried in Monument Cemetery, which later became Chalmette National Cemetery. The location of Private Wakeman's grave was confirmed in a September, 1992 phone call to Gary Hume, Superintendent, Chalmette National Cemetery, U.S. National Park Service.

APPENDIX A

History of the 153rd Regiment
New York State Volunteers

August 1862 - October 18, 1862

The 153rd Regiment, New York State Volunteers, was organized in Herkimer County, New York, Col. Duncan McMartin commanding. Capt. George H. McLaughlin recruited Company G, later designated Company H, near Fonda, New York. The regiment was mustered into service on October 17, 1862, and left New York state on October 18th for duty in Washington City.

October 1862 - February 2, 1863

Stationed in Alexandria, Virginia, the 153rd was assigned guard and provost marshall duty. They were placed under the command of Col. Clarence Buell (169th NYSV), who headed the Provisional Brigade to which the 153rd was attached, in Abercrombie's Division, Defenses of Washington, under the overall command of Maj. Gen. Nathaniel P. Banks.

February 2, 1863 - July 20, 1863

The Regiment was reassigned to the District of Alexandria under the command of Brig. Gen. John Potts Slough. The soldiers of the 153rd took up residence in Camp Slough west of Alexandria, one of many temporary troop camps located in the outer defenses of the Capital City. They performed guard and provost marshal duty in Alexandria and the surrounding area. Included in their duties were Grand Guard, Hunting Creek, Alexandria City Patrol, City Provost Marshal office (Gen. J.P. Slough's office), Alexandria Jail, the Water Battery, the Contraband Depot, and, curiously enough, "Miss Elliot's Garden." Colonel McMartin resigned due to ill health and Maj. Edwin P. Davis was promoted to colonel commanding the 153rd on May 1, 1863.

July 20, 1863 - February 18, 1864

Transferred to Washington City and to the command of Brig. Gen. John Henry Martindale, the 153rd moved into barracks on Capitol Hill as unattached troops in the 22nd Army Corps, Department of Washington. The New Yorkers stood guard at the Old Capitol and Carroll Prisons on Capitol Hill, and at City Hall, the Central Guard House, Camp Baker, and the B & O Railroad Depot.

February 16-19, 1864

The 153rd received marching orders instructing them to go to Alexandria, Virginia for transport to Louisiana on the steamship *Mississippi*. They stayed at the Soldiers' Rest in Alexandria for two days prior to their departure.

February 20-29, 1864

The steamship *Mississippi* departed on the 20th for the nine-day voyage to the City of Algiers, opposite New Orleans on the banks of the Mississippi River.

March 1-14, 1864

From Algiers, the 153rd traveled west to Brashear City by rail and marched 53 miles to Franklin, arriving sometime before the 8th of March. They were then assigned to the veteran First Brigade, command of Brig. Gen. William Dwight; First Division, command of Brig. Gen. William H. Emory; 19th Army Corps, Maj. Gen. William Buell Franklin; Department of the Gulf, command of Maj. Gen. Nathaniel Prentiss Banks. For several days most of the army was kept ignorant of the objective of their upcoming campaign, and rumors circulated that they would go to Mobile, Alabama. They were, however, preparing for hard campaigning in the Red River region of Louisiana. The object of this campaign was to take Shreveport, the Confederate state capitol of Louisiana at the head of navigation of the Red River, as a staging point for an expedition into Texas.

March 15-20, 1864

The 19th Army Corps, accompanied by the 13th Corps and a division of cavalry under Brig. Gen. Albert L. Lee, began its journey north up the Bayou Teche. One veteran of the Louisiana campaigns under Banks wrote that "the Teche country was to the war in Louisiana what the Shenandoah Valley was to the war in Virginia," but that "There the resemblance ends, for the Teche country is a long flat, hemmed in by marshes and bayous."[1] The Louisiana Confederate state government retired along this same route in the face of previous Federal movements, locating first at Opelousas, then Alexandria to the north, and finally settling in Shreveport near the Texas border.

The army set out on March 15 and averaged 16 miles a day, making its way to Washington, Louisiana, and building a bridge over Vermilion Bayou on the way. A march of 19 miles on March

18 "was one of great severity and fatigue, and caused much straggling among the newly enlisted Regiments that were making their first campaign. It was painful to witness the young and pale-faced recruits, whose stiffened limbs and blistered feet could scarcely drag their tired bodies along."[2] They rested at Washington on the 20th, having covered 80 miles in the five previous days.

March 21-27, 1864

The 153rd's journey was resumed in a "cold, drizzling rain" on March 21st, which kept the army to only 12 miles for the day.[3] The army's line of march diverged from the banks of the Bayou Teche and began to follow the Bayou Boeuf. They camped at Holmesville on the 22nd after an 18-mile day, journeyed 15 miles on the 23rd to Cheneyville, and another 18 miles the following day before they slept in the rain on the grounds of the Wells Plantation the night of the 24th. M.J. Wells, owner of the property, was serving as the Free-State Lieutenant Governor of Louisiana at the time.

On the 24th it was learned that Brig. Gen. A.J. Smith's troops had reduced and captured Fort De Russy, leaving Alexandria open to the Federals.[4] A short trek on the 25th brought the 19th and 13th Corps to the town of Alexandria on the Red River. After resting briefly outside of the town, General Franklin's troops marched down the main street of Alexandria in review before General Banks, the regimental bands playing and their state and national colors unfurled. North of town the army camped by the banks of the Bayou Rapides, where they stayed for two days.

Here Franklin's troops were joined by the 16th and 17th Corps under General Smith, on loan from General Sherman's army, as well as by a large naval fleet of ironclads, gunboats, and transports under the command of R. Adm. David Porter. The river transports carried food, ammunition, and forage for the army, which could not subsist off the land in the sandy pine forest country they were about to enter.

March 28-April 4, 1864

March 28 dawned with a 19th Corps movement up the Red River, preceded by miles of wagons that cut up the roads and made it difficult for the troops to march. On March 29 the Union cavalry division engaged and defeated a small Confederate force on Henderson's Bluff. March 31 brought Banks' army to its first crossing of the Cane River, a stagnant old channel of the Red River. The 18-mile march of that day was "especially disagreeable...high wind filled the air with dust."[5]

Another 18-mile trek on April 1 took them across the Cane River again. The next day they reached Natchitoches, and five miles beyond it, Grand Ecore Landing. At Grand Ecore the supplies the army needed for the next leg of its journey were unloaded from Admiral Porter's transports, as Banks planned to leave the river and swing west, to take advantage of the best road to Shreveport. Admiral Porter's fleet was to continue, unprotected by infantry, up the Red River.

April 5-8, 1864

General Banks toured the camps at Grand Ecore on April 5, and that evening the band of the 153rd New York serenaded the army.[6] The combined force of Lee's cavalry, the 19th and 13th Corps, and Brig. Gen. A. J. Smith's 16th and 17th Corps numbered approximately 45,000 soldiers. With this force and Porter's fleet, Banks expected to travel another 90 miles north, take Shreveport, establish a strong garrison and defenses to hold the town, and then return General Smith's troops to Sherman in time to commence the spring general offensive planned by Lt. Gen. U.S. Grant.

On the 6th, Banks' army began its final movement toward Shreveport, marching 18 miles. The following day brought the army to Pleasant Hill, described as "the largest clearing we have met in the Piney Woods, on a beautiful mound.... This is one of the favorite summer resorts of the wealthy.... We are told that in peace-times it was the scene of luxury and fashion, and that the woods were made to ring with music and dancing."[7]

April 8 saw the 13th Corps pass in front of the 19th along the narrow road through the dense pine forest. At three o'clock in the afternoon the 19th bivouacked in a clearing by the road. But the sound of artillery was heard toward the front, and the Corps was ordered to fall in quickly and move forward.

At Mansfield, Confederate troops under Maj. Gen. Richard Taylor, son of former President Zachary Taylor, had attacked the Union cavalry in the van of the march, capturing the cavalry wagons and two artillery batteries. Men of the 13th Corps were ordered up to support the cavalry, but "there was little use in a division of cavalry seven or eight thousand strong, and about five thousand infantry, trying to drive back an army of twenty-five to thirty thousand."[8] No match for the victorious Confederate onslaught, the broken Union troops fled back down the woods-bordered road. The 19th Corps was ordered forward, formed front in a line of battle in a clearing in the woods, and repulsed Taylor's attack. Darkness brought a halt to further engagement. The 153rd New York was detached from the First Brigade during the fight to relieve the 30th Maine and guard the supply train to the rear.[9]

In the cold evening the 19th Corps watched and waited until midnight for further Confederate movements. Then, convinced that the enemy would make no further forays, the 19th Corps commenced an eight-mile retreat to Pleasant Hill, the 153rd rejoining the First Brigade en route.

April 9-10, 1864

The 19th Corps reached Pleasant Hill in the early morning and was ordered into line of battle to await a follow up attack by the Confederates. The 153rd New York, stationed with the First Brigade, held the center of the 19th's line of battle. The 16th and 17th Corps formed in their rear as reserves, with the 13th assigned to guard the wagon train several miles back.

"At 4:30 o'clock, precisely, the Rebel cavalry advanced toward the right and center, the exultant foe yelling in the most fiendish manner, at the same time brandishing their sabres in the air," according to one veteran of the battle of Pleasant Hill.[10] Under command of General Emory, the 19th Corps beat a slow, fighting retreat up the slope of Pleasant Hill, then filed off to the left when they reached the crest. As two Confederate lines of battle emerged over the crest of the hill, Union forces arrayed to the rear opened a terrible fire that devastated the gray ranks. The order to charge was given and the 19th Corps joined the rush to the enemy lines. Triumphant, the Federals drove Taylor's remaining troops off the hill and down into the woods. The Union troops pursued fleeing Confederates, recaptured their artillery batteries, and took 500 prisoners, three stands of colors, a large number of small arms, and all of the dead and wounded.

Darkness brought a cessation of hostilities. The 153rd lay on their arms on the field of battle to await orders, and to help the wounded as far as possible. Casualties for the 153rd during its first test under fire were 1 killed, 28 wounded, and 12 missing.

At midnight, April 9, orders were given to the Federals to fall back to Grand Ecore on the Red River. The army had lost contact with its supply trains and was now in dire need of food, forage, and water, all of which was scarce in the Pleasant Hill vicinity. After three days and nights with no rest, having marched over 50 miles and engaged in its first major battle, all with little or nothing to eat, the 153rd trudged back to Grand Ecore Landing before dawn.

April 11-22, 1864

Banks' army arrived at Grand Ecore on the 11th, entrenched, and went into bivouac to rest and resupply. Banks wished to continue the campaign, but the water level of the Red River was falling, imperiling Admiral Porter's fleet. The deadline for returning Brig. Gen. A.J. Smith's troops to Sherman had passed. Finally, on the 20th, the Federal command learned that Taylor's force had gotten around to their rear down the river. This news forced Banks to abandon any forward movement and to make a final retreat down the Red to the Mississippi.

The retreat began at 10 o'clock in the evening of the 21st. While burning houses and cotton bales illuminated the night along their route, Banks' army marched until dawn and through all of the next day, covering 35 miles by midnight of the 22nd.

April 23-25, 1864

After only a few short hours of rest, the Federals resumed their forced march at 4 a.m. on the 23rd. At sunrise they arrived at Monett's Bluff, one of two Cane River crossings along their route. Across the river the Confederates confronted them, with infantry and artillery posted on a high bank. While the Third Brigade was instructed to move up the river three miles, ford the stream, and proceed back down the river to attack the Rebel force on its left flank, the 153rd, along with the First Brigade, was posted just across the river below the bluff in a stand of trees. Sounds of cannonading five miles to the Union rear notified all within hearing that a large Confederate force had fallen upon General Smith's rear guard. Banks' army was surrounded and trapped.

While posted in the trees by the river, waiting for their comrades to attack the Confederate left, the 153rd was subjected to a constant artillery bombardment. After several anxious hours they heard the sounds of the detached Federal Third Brigade assaulting the Rebel force. A fierce battle ensued, lasting an hour. When it appeared that the Union troops had turned the Confederate left, the 153rd's brigade was ordered up and into a wild charge on the enemy. By the time they had crossed over the river, though, the First Brigade found the Rebels broken and fleeing. At the same time, the distant roar of artillery in the army's rear ceased, signaling Smith's victory over Taylor's attack on the Federal rear guard.

The 153rd acquitted itself well in its second engagement, but had little time to rejoice and regroup. Within an hour of the battle at Monett's Bluff, engineers had constructed a pontoon bridge over the Cane, and the army passed over the river to continue its forced march until midnight of the 23rd. Two more days of grueling marching lay ahead of them before they reached Alexandria, Louisiana.

April 26-May 12, 1864
At Alexandria, the army rested while the enemy threatened it with constant skirmishing on the picket lines. The Red River had fallen so low that it appeared Admiral Porter's fleet might be abandoned because it could not negotiate the rapids above Alexandria. But on May 4, army engineers came to the rescue of the navy by building a wing-dam on the river to raise the water level above the rough water, allowing the fleet to safely shoot the rapids once the wings were opened. Construction of the dam took eight days.

On May 12 the dam was completed. Admiral Porter's fleet passed safely through the deep channel created when the wings of the dam were opened, and proceeded down the Red.

May 13-21, 1864
The army resumed its retreat to the Mississippi, skirmishing with the enemy every step of the way. The 153rd took part in the fighting of the Battle of Mansura on May 15-16, and the Engagement at Avoyelle's Prairie on the 16th. The Red River campaign ended on May 21, when the 153rd reached Morganza on the Mississippi River, above Port Hudson.

May 21-July 1, 1864
With the 19th and 13th Corps, the 153rd was garrisoned at Morganza. At this juncture, Brig. Gen. A.J. Smith's 16th and 17th Corps parted ways with Banks' command.

July 1-12, 1864
The 19th Army Corps was transferred to the Eastern theater of operations, and embarked for Washington City via Fort Monroe, Virginia. The 153rd was not allowed to disembark from the transports at Fort Monroe, however. Instead, General Grant ordered the 19th to Washington to defend the city against an impending attack by a Confederate force under Lt. Gen. Jubal Early.

July 13-14, 1864
The 153rd arrived in Washington City and marched north to Fort Stevens, which was threatened by Early's command. While

engaged in sharp exchanges of fire with the enemy, troops defending the fort were visited by President Lincoln, who wished to view a battle first hand. This was the only time that Lincoln observed a battle in the Civil War. Early's troops retreated once they learned that they were confronted with the veterans of the 6th and 19th Corps rather than the untested 100-day regiments they had hoped to find defending Washington.

July 14-23, 1864
With the 19th Army Corps, the 153rd struck west in pursuit of Early's command, following the Rebel force through Snicker's Gap and into the Shenandoah Valley in Virginia.

August 7-November 28, 1864
United with Maj. Gen. Philip Sheridan's command in the Shenandoah Valley, the 153rd took part in Sheridan's 1864 Valley Campaign. The Regiment was engaged in the Third Battle of Winchester, Virginia on September 19; the Battle of Fisher's Hill on September 22; and the Battle of Cedar Creek on October 19. This last marked the destruction of Early's force as an effective command and a hindrance to the operations of Union troops in the Shenandoah.

Col. Edwin P. Davis was recognized for his "gallant and meritorious service" during these battles, and was given command of the Second Brigade, 19th Army Corps in October before taking leave to recover from a battle wound. In February of 1865 he was breveted brigadier general and given command of the Subdistrict of Ogeechee (near Savannah, GA), Department of the South. George H. McLaughlin, captain of Co. H, 153rd New York, also was promoted, serving as lieutenant colonel commanding the regiment during this period.

November 28, 1864-April 5, 1865
The 153rd was assigned duty at Middletown, Newtown, and Stephenson's Depot in Virginia until being transferred to Washington City on April 5.

April 6-July, 1865
After a year and a half away, the 153rd resumed duty in Washington City. The regiment took part in the Grand Review of the Armies on May 23, celebrating the end of the War of Rebellion. This massive parade down Pennsylvania Avenue of both eastern and western Federal armies took two days. They passed in review

before the nation's new President, Andrew Johnson, who was sworn into office shortly after President Lincoln's assassination on April 14, 1865.

July-October 2, 1865

The 153rd was transferred to the Department of Georgia and was stationed at Savannah, Georgia. On October 2, 1865, the regiment was mustered out of service. During its service, the 153rd lost 1 officer and 38 enlisted men killed or mortally wounded in battle, and 1 officer and 160 enlisted men due to disease. Total casualties came to 200, or approximately 20 percent of the regiment's original strength.

Notes

1. John W. DeForest, "The Confederates Escape in the Teche Country," in Henry Steel Commanger, *The Blue & the Gray,* Vol. I, (Indianapolis: Bobbs-Merrill Company, 1950), p. 474.

2. Beecher, p. 294.

3. Pellet, p. 178.

4. Pellet, p. 180.

5. Beecher, p. 305.

6. Pellet, p. 193.

7. Pellet, p. 193

8. Clark, p. 155.

9. Beecher, pg. 312; Henry N. Fairbanks, "The Red River Expedition of 1864," Vol. II, *War Papers Read to the Maine Commandery, Military Order of the Loyal Legion of the U.S.,* (Portland, ME: Lefavor-Tower Co., 1902), p. 181.

10. Flinn, pp. 112-113.

ORDERS OF BATTLE
153rd Regiment, New York State Volunteers

October 18, 1862--February 2, 1863
Defenses of Washington
Maj. Gen. Nathaniel Prentiss Banks

Abercrombie's Division
Brig. Gen. John Joseph Abercrombie

Provisional Brigade
Col. Clarence Buell, 169th New York

119th New York
152nd New York
153rd New York
169th New York

February 2, 1863--July 20, 1863
District of Alexandria
Brig. Gen. John Potts Slough

1st District of Columbia
23rd Maine
26th Michigan
153rd New York
11th Rhode Island
Independent Battery H, Pennsylvania Light
  Artillery

July 20, 1863--February 18, 1864
XXII Army Corps, Department of Washington
Maj. Gen. Samuel P. Heintzelman through October 13, 1863
Maj. Gen. Christopher Columbus Augur

Martindale's Command
Maj. Gen. John Henry Martindale

Unattached Troops
153rd New York

February 18, 1864--July 1, 1864
Department of the Gulf
Maj. Gen. Nathaniel Prentiss Banks

XIX Army Corps
Maj. Gen. Wm. B. Franklin through May 2, 1864
Brig. Gen. William Hemsley Emory

1st Division
Brig. Gen. William H. Emory through May 2, 1864.
Brig. Gen. James W. McMillan through June 25, 1864
Brig. Gen. Benjamin Stone Roberts

1st Brigade
Brig. Gen. William Dwight through Feb. 2, 1864
Col. George M. Love, 116th NY,through March 25, 1864
Brig. Gen. William Dwight through April 18, 1864.
Col. George Beal, 29th Maine

29th Maine
20th Massachusetts
114th New York
116th New York
153rd New York
161st New York

July 1, 1864--March 20, 1865
Army of the Shenandoah
Maj. Gen. Philip Henry Sheridan

XIX Army Corps
Brig. Gen. William H. Emory

1st Division
Brig. Gen. William Dwight
(relieved occasionally by Brig. Gen. James W. McMillan)

1st Brigade
Col. George L. Beale, 29th Maine through October 13, 1864
Col. Edwin P. Davis, 153rd NY through October 30, 1864
Col. George M. Love, 116th NY through November 1, 1864
Col. N.A.M. Dudley, 30th MA through December 13, 1864
Brig. Gen. George L. Beale through March 20, 1865

        29th Maine
        30th Massachusetts
        90th New York
        114th New York
        116th New York
        153rd New York

March 20, 1865--April 5, 1865
Army of the Shenandoah
Maj. Gen. Alfred T. A. Torbert

  1st Provisional Division
  Bvt. Maj. Gen. James McMillan

    2nd Brigade
    Col. Edwin P. Davis, 153rd New York

        12th Connecticut
        15th Maine
        153rd New York
        47th Pennsylvania
        8th Vermont

April 5--July, 1865
XXII Army Corps, Department of Washington
Maj. Gen. Christopher Columbus Augur

  Dwight's Division
  Brig. Gen. William Dwight

        2nd Brigade
        12th Connecticut
        15th Maine
        153rd New York
        47th Pennsylvania
        8th Vermont

July, 1865--October 2, 1865
Department of the South
Maj. Gen. Quincy Adams Gillmore

        Unattached Troops
        153rd New York

APPENDIX B

Wakeman Genealogy

116. Harvey Anable Wakeman, of Afton, N. Y., married at Coventry, NY., April 4, 1842, Emily Hale (b. March 18, 1823; d. April 3, 1884), daughter of William Hale and Sarah Baker. They begat,

I. Sarah Rosetta. b. Jan 16, 1843, d. June 19, 1864 at New Orleans, La.

II. Emily Celestia, B. March 12, 1847, She m. in Guilford, N. Y., May 17, 1871, Leonard John Montgomery, of Colesville and Bainbridge, N. Y. (b. June 20, 1847). They begat,
    A. George Wakeman, B. Aug. 13, 1875.
    B. Fred Leonard, b. Nov. 8, 1886.

III. Lois Amelia, B. Aug. 17, 1849; d. March 11, 1876. She m. at Port Crane, N. Y., Oct. 3, 1869, Bradley Henry Bates (b. June 3, 1859(, and begat
    A. George Henry, b. Oct. 10, 1870.
    B. Luella May, b. Jan. 27, 1876.

IV. Robert Etna, B. Aug. 14, 1851; d. Dec. 21, 1896.

V. Susan Althea, b. July 28, 1853; d. April 13, 1876. She m. at Doraville, N. Y., April 20, 1873, Alva Jackson Wilder, of Bainbridge, N. Y. (b. July 6, 1842). They begat,
    A. Lewis A., b. March 10, 1874.
    B. Susie L., b. April 6, 1876. She m. Jan 15, 1896 Guy Blowers, of N. Sanford, N.Y. (b. June 15, 1870).
    C. Dayton Edwin, b. Feb. 15, 1886; d. July 28, 1886.

VI. Sophronia Angelia, b. April 21, 1855. She m. at Harpersville, Jan. 21, 1873, Edwin Clendenning, of Coventry, N. Y. (b. May 22, 1851; d. July 1, 1880). They begat,
    A. Della M., b. April 9, 1875. She m. Dec. 28, 1894, LeRoy McCulley (b. April 11, 1873), and begat, Lina Roxena, b. March 2, 1897.

VII. Mary Eda Alvira, b. Feb. 27, 1858. She m. at E. Windsor, NY, Jan. 2, 1888, Avery Stillson, of Doraville, NY (b. April 8, 1822; d. May 6, 1897.)

VIII. Harvey Lincoln, b. Dec. 4, 1861.

IX. Catharine Elizabeth, b. Jan 19, 1863. She m. at Coventry, N. Y., Oct. 5, 1881, Albert Leroy Smith (b. Sept. 12, 1858). They begat,
> A. Mabel Elizabeth, b. June 16, 1883; d. Aug. 15, 1883.
> B. Ruth Emily, b. March 2, 1885.
> C. Neva Ida, b. Oct. 21, 1893.
> D. Esther Elizabeth, b. March 4, 1898.

Bibliography

Primary Sources

Published Materials:
Beecher, Dr. Harris H. *Record of the 114th Regiment, New York State Volunteers: Where it Went, What it Saw, and What it Did.* Norwich, NY: J. F. Hubbard, Jr., 1866.

Boyd, Belle. *In Camp and Prison.* London: Saunders, Otley & Co., 1865.

Clark, Orton S. *The 116th Regiment of New York State Volunteers.* Buffalo, NY: Matthew & Warren, 1868.

De Forest, John William, (James Croushore, ed.). *A Volunteer's Adventures: A Union Captain's Record of the Civil War.* New Haven, CT: Yale University Press, 1946.

Early, Jubal Anderson. *Jubal Early's Memoirs: Autobiographical Sketch and Narrative of the War Between the States.* Baltimore, MD: The N&A Publishing Co., 1989.

Edmonds, S. Emma E. *Nurse and Spy.* Hartford, CT: W.S. Williams & Co., 1865.

Fairbanks, Henry N. "The Red River Expedition of 1864," Vol. II, *War Papers Read before the Maine Commandery, Military Order of the Loyal Legion of the United States.* Portland, ME: Lefavor-Tower Co., 1902.

Flinn, Frank M. *Campaigning with Banks in Louisiana.* Lynn, MA: Thos. P. Nichols, 1887.

Gardner, Ira B. *Recollections of a Boy Member of the Maine 14th.* Lewiston, ME: Lewiston Journal Co., 1906.

Howe, Henry Warren. *Passages from the Life of Henry Warren Howe, Consisting of Diary and Letters Written During the Civil War, 1861-1865, Condensed History of the Thirtieth Massachusetts Regiment.* Lowell, MA: Courier-Citizen Co., 1899.

Irwin, Richard B., "The Red River Campaign," Vol. IV. *Battles and Leaders of the Civil War.* Secaucus, NJ: Castle, [1883] 1989.

Jones, William E. *The Military History of the 161st New York Volunteers.* Bath, NY: N.p., 1865.

Livermore, Mary. *My Story of the War.* Hartford, CT: A.D. Worthington & Co., 1888.

Pellet, Elias Porter. *History of the 114th Regiment, New York State Volunteers.* Norwich, NY: Telegraph & Chronicle Power Press, 1866.

Sheridan, Phillip H. *Personal Memoirs of P.H. Sheridan.* New York: Charles Webster & Company, 1888.

Shorey, Henry Augustus. *Story of the Maine 15th.* Bridgton, ME: Press of the Bridgton News, 1890.

Smith, E. Kirby. "The Defense of the Red River." Vol. IV, *Battles and Leaders of the Civil War.* Secaucus, NJ: Castle, [1883] 1989.

Taylor, Richard. *Destruction and Reconstruction: Personal Reminiscences of the Late War.* New York, NY: D. Appleton & Company, 1879.

Williamson, James Joseph. *Prison Life in the Old Capitol and Reminiscences of the Civil War.* West Orange, NJ: N.p., 1911.

Wittenmyer, Annie. *Under the Guns: A Woman's Reminiscences of the Civil War.* Boston, MA: Stillings & Co, 1895.

Unpublished Sources:

Eighteenth Annual Reunion of the 153rd N.Y. Veteran Association, 1899, proceedings. Montgomery County Department of History and Archives, Fonda, NY.

Enders, Rev. Jacob H., 153rd New York Infantry. *Letters, 1862-1881.* Montgomery Department of History and Archives, Fonda, NY.

Forty-Fifth Re-Union, 115th & 153rd Regiments, New York Vol. Infantry, held at Amsterdam, NY, August 26, 1925, proceedings. Montgomery County Department of History and Archives, Fonda, NY.

Hodges, Lt. George H. *Record of the 153rd New York State Infantry, read by Lt. George H. Hodges at the Tenth Annual Re-Union of the 153rd N.Y. Veteran Association, September 17, 1891, at Greenfield Centre, Saratoga Co., New York.* Montgomery County Department of History and Archives, Fonda, NY.

Lassell, Pvt. John (James F. Morrison, ed.). *The Boys in Blue of Co., 153rd New York State Volunteers, Civil War Diary of John Lassell.* Montgomery Department of History and Archives, Fonda, NY.

Root, Col. Adrian, 94th New York State Volunteers. *Letter, April 5, 1863.* Courtesy of Benedict R. Maryniak, Buffalo, NY.

Smith, Neva Ida. *Letters, 1976.* Courtesy of Mrs. Ruth Goodier, Chipley, FL.

Wilder, Burl H. *Wilder Genealogy.* Courtesy of Mrs. Ruth Goodier, Chipley, FL.

U.S. Government Publications & Records:

The War of the Rebellion: A Compilation of the Official Records of the Union and Confederate Armies, Series I, Vol. 34,

Parts I, II, and III. Washington, D.C.: U.S. Government Printing Office, 1880-1901.

U.S. Census Records, 1850. Chenango County, New York, Town of Bainbridge. National Archives.

U.S. Census Records, 1860. Chenango County, New York, Town of Afton. National Archives.

U.S. War Department. *Revised Regulations for the Army of the United States.* Philadelphia: J.G.L. Brown, 1861.

Record Group 15, Records of the Veteran's Administration, Civil War Pension Application Files, National Archives:

> *File No. C-2, 573248, Pvt. Albert D.J. Cashier, Company G, 95th Illinois Infantry.*

> *File No. SC 153.669, Edwin P. Davis, Captain in the 64th Regiment, New York State Volunteers, and Colonel commanding the 153rd New York State Volunteers.*

> *File No. SC 222.100, Pvt. Frank R. Roberts, Company D, 64th New York Infantry.*

> *File No. SC 282.136, Pvt. Franklin Thompson, Company F, 2nd Michigan Infantry.*

> *File No. SC 381.202, Pvt. Perry A. Wilder, 109th New York Infantry.*

Record Group 94, Records of the Adjutant General's Office, 1780-1917, Compiled Military Service Records, National Archives:

> *Pvt. Asa L. Austin, 64th New York Infantry.*

> *Pvt. Phillip N. Austin, 64th New York Infantry.*

> *Sgt. William Henry Austin, 109th New York Inf.*

> *Pvt. Albert D.J. Cashier, 95th Illinois Infantry.*

> *Col. Edwin P. Davis, 153rd New York Infantry. Captain, 62nd Regiment, New York Infantry.*

> *Capt. George H. McLaughlin, Company G, later H, 153rd New York Infantry.*

> *Pvt. William B. Parsons, 64th New York Infantry.*

> *Pvt. Frank R. Roberts, Company D, 64th New York Infantry.*

> *Pvt. Henry Saunders, 5th Wisconsin Infantry.*

> *Pvt. Hiram Sweet, 153rd New York Infantry.*

> *Pvt. Franklin Thompson, 2nd Michigan Volunteer Infantry.*

> *Pvt. Lyons Wakeman, Company G, later H, 153rd New York Infantry.*

*Pvt. Gilbert Warren, Company G, later H, 153rd
New York Infantry.*

Pvt. John Webb, 153rd New York Infantry.

Pvt. Perry A. Wilder, 109th New York Infantry.

*Pvt. Stephen Wiley, Company G, later H, 153rd
New York Infantry.*

Record Group 94, Carded Medical Records, Volunteers,
Mexican & Civil Wars, 1846-1865, National Archives:

*Pvt. Ransom Conklin, Company H, 153rd New
York Infantry.*

*Pvt. Albert Weathermax, Company H, 153rd New
York Infantry.*

*Pvt. Lyons Wakeman, Company H, 153rd New York
Infantry.*

*Pvt. Edwin West, Company H, 153rd New York
Infantry.*

Record Group 94, Records of the 153rd New York Infantry,
National Archives:

Regimental Descriptive Books.

Regimental Order Books.

Regimental Letter Books.

Record Group 393, Records of the U.S. Army Continental
Commands, Carroll Prison Records, Vol. 329, National Archives:

Carroll Prison Guard Reports, 1863.

Discharge Records for Carroll Prison, 1864 & 1865.

State Government Records:

New York: 1865 Census. *List of death of officers and enlisted
men that occurred while in military or naval service of the U.S. or
from wound or disease acquired in said service since April 1861,
reported to families to which deceased belonged when at home in
the Town of Afton.* Office of the Chenango County Clerk, Norwich,
New York.

Journal article:

Hodges, Robert Jr., (Darst, Maury, ed.). "Robert Hodges, Jr.,
Confederate Soldier," *East Texas Historical Journal.* Vol. 9,
No. 1.

Secondary Sources

Books

Anthony, Susan B., Matilda Gage and Elizabeth Cady Stanton.
History of Women's Suffrage. 6 Vols. New York: Fowler & Wells,
1882.

Beers & Co., F. W. *History of Montgomery and Fulton Counties.* New York: Geo. McNamara, Printer, 1878.

Beyer, Barry K. *The Chenango Canal.* New York: The Chenango County Historical Society, 1990.

Casey, Powell A. *Encyclopedia of Forts, Posts, Named Camps, & Other Military Installations in Louisiana, 1700-1981.* Baton Rouge, LA: Claitor's Publishing Division, 1981.

Coco, Gregory A. *On the Bloodstained Field.* Wheatfield Press, 1987.

Cooling, Benjamin and Walton H. Owen. *Mr. Lincoln's Forts.* Shippensburg, PA: White Mane Publishing Co., 1988.

Cooling, Benjamin. *Symbol, Sword, and Shield: Defending Washington During the Civil War.* Shippensburg, PA: White Mane Publishing Co., second revised ed., 1991.

Cornish, Dudley Taylor. *The Sable Arm: Black Troops in the Union Army, 1861-1865.* Univ. Press of Kansas, [1956]1987 .

Dannett, Sylvia. *She Rode with the Generals.* New York: Thomas Nelson & Sons, 1960.

Dyer, Frederick H. *A Compendium of the War of Rebellion Compiled and Arranged from Official Records of the Federal and Confederate Armies, Reports of the Adjutant Generals of the Several States, the Army Registers and Other Reliable Documents and Sources.* 3 Vols. New York: Thomas Yoseloff, [1908]1959.

Kirkland, Fazar. *Reminiscences of the Blue and Gray, '61 to '65.* Chicago: Preston Publishing Company, 1895.

Jones, Katherine M. *Heroines of Dixie.* New York: Bobbs-Merrill, 1955.

Jordan, Weymouth T., Jr. *North Carolina Troops, 1861-1865: A Roster.* 13 Vols. Raleigh, NC: North Carolina Division of Archives & History, 1987.

McPherson, James M. *The Negro in the Civil War.* New York: Vintage Books, 1965.

Moneyhan, Carl and Bobby Roberts. *Portraits of Conflict: A Photographic History of Louisiana in the Civil War.* The Univ. of Arkansas Press, 1990.

Moore, Madeline. *The Lady Lieutenant: The Strange and Thrilling Adventures of Miss Madeline Moore.* Philadelphia: Barclay & Co., 1862.

Pryor, Elizabeth Brown. *Clara Barton: Professional Angel.* Philadelphia: Univ. of Pennsylvania Press, 1987.

Quarles, Benjamin. *The Negro in the Civil War.* New York: Da Capo Press, 1953.

Robertson, James I. *Soldiers Blue & Gray.* Univ. of South Carolina Press, 1988.

Smith, Mrs. Edwin P. *Vital Records of Chenango County, NY, Before 1880.* Norwich, NY: Chenango County Historical Society, 1975.

Smith, James A. *History of Chenango and Madison Counties.* Syracuse, NY: D. Mason & Co., 1880.

Wakeman, Robert P. *Wakeman Genealogy, 1630-1899.* Meriden, CT: Journal Publishing Co., 1900.

Wakeman, Thomas H. *Wakeman Genealogy II, Sequel to Wakeman Genealogy (1900).* 2 Vols. Baltimore, MD: Gateway Press, 1989.

Wheelwright, Julie. *Amazons & Military Maids: Women Who Dressed as Men in the Pursuit of Life, Liberty, & Happiness.* London: Pandora Press, 1989.

Wiley, Bell I. *Confederate Women.* Westport, CT: Greenwood Press, 1975.

Wiley, Bell I. *The Life of Billy Yank, the Common Soldier of the Union.* Louisiana State Univ. Press, [1952] 1971.

Velasquez, Loreta Janeta. *The Woman in Battle.* Hartford, CT: T. Belknap, 1876.

Newspaper article:

Fonda, NY *Morning Herald,* Thursday, September 17, 1914. "History of the 153rd Regiment, New York State Volunteers."

Index